# ON T [illegible] )

SAINT BERNARD OF CLAIRVAUX

AETERNA PRESS

PUBLISHED BY AETERNA PRESS.
COVER DESIGN BY AETERNA PRESS.

TEXT TRANSLATED BY MARIANNE CAROLINE AND COVENTRY PATMORE

SECOND EDITION

LONDON BURNS AND OATES 1884

PREFATORY NOTE MY WIFE WAS OCCUPIED ON THIS TRANSLATION AT THE TIME OF HER DEATH. PP. 1–98 INCLUDE HER WORK; THE REST IS MINE. COVENTRY PATMORE. HASTINGS, FEBRUARY 10, 1881.

ISBN-13: 978-1-78516-105-6

AVAILABLE AS AN E-BOOK:
WWW.AETERNAPRESS.COM

# CONTENTS

# A LITTLE WORK BY ST. BERNARD ON THE LOVE OF GOD

## CHAPTER I

### WHY WE OUGHT TO LOVE GOD, AND HOW WE OUGHT TO LOVE HIM

YOU wish me to explain for what reason and in what measure we should love God.

I should say that God Himself is the motive of our love to Him, and that the measure of due love is to be without measure. Is this clear enough? Perhaps it may be for a person of intelligence, but I desire to answer for both the learned and unlearned; and, though I may have said enough for the former, I must remember others also. For them I will unfold my meaning, and perhaps add somewhat to it.

Two things there are that move us to love God for Himself: nothing is more reasonable; nothing is more profitable.

The question, What binds us to love God? may either mean—What is His title to our love? or, How will it profit us to love God? To both these forms of the question there is but one answer: The motive for loving God, is God. No title can be stronger than this: God gave Himself to us in spite of our unworthiness, and, being God, what could He give us of greater worth than Himself? If, then, by asking, why we are bound to love God, we mean, what is His claim, the answer is: Especially this, that He first loved us. This gives Him a right to our love in return; above all, considering who He is that loves, what His loved ones are, and in what way He loves them. For who is He that loves us, but He of whom every spirit bears witness: "Thou art my God, Thou hast no need of my goods"? and His love is it not that charity that seeks not its own interests? But on whom is fastened this unselfish love? The Apostle answers: "When we were yet enemies, we were reconciled to God." God has loved us disinterestedly, and while yet we were His enemies. But how has He loved us?

St. John says to this extreme: "God so loved the world as to give His only begotten Son." St. Paul adds: "He hath not spared His only begotten Son, but hath delivered Him up for us;" and the Son says of Himself, "Greater love hath no man than this, that a man lay down his life for his friends." These are the claims which God, the Holy, the sovereignly great and Almighty, has upon the love of infinitely little, weak, and sinful man. It may be said: Yes, this is true of mankind, but it is not so of angels. I know it; for angels the same was not needful. Moreover, He who has helped man in his misery preserved the angels from falling into the like; and if God's love for men has found them a way of escape, it is by the self-same that He kept the angels from a fall like ours.

## CHAPTER II

### THAT GOD HAS A RIGHT TO THE LOVE OF MAN BECAUSE OF HIS GIFTS TO SOUL AND BODY. HOW THESE SHOULD BE CONFESSED, AND NOT TURNED AGAINST HIM WHO GAVE THEM

THOSE who have acknowledged what I have said must surely own our obligation to love God. But if there be infidels who will not do so much, God has wherewith to confound their ingratitude in the goods beyond number with which He enriches soul and body. Is it not from Him that man receives the bread which sustains, the light which enlightens him, the air which he breathes? If I mention these first, it is not that I account them chief, for they only concern the body, but they are the most necessary. For our chief goods we must look into the soul, the superior part of our being. Those goods are—excellence, intelligence, and virtue. When I speak of excellence in man, I mean the free will which is in him, it being this which lifts him above all other living beings and places them under his dominion. Intelligence proves to him his excellence, and at the same time proves that he owes it not to himself; and, lastly, virtue makes him seek ardently, and when he has found, embrace vehemently, Him whose work he is.

These three goods present each of them two aspects. Excellence is seen as the prerogative proper to human nature, and also as causing that fear which man has always produced in every other living being. Intelligence perceives the dignity of man, but at the same time owns that though in him, yet it is not of him; and, lastly, virtue in its double action provokes to an eager seeking for Him to whom we owe existence, and, when found, as eager a clinging to Him. Moreover, excellence without intelligence is worthless; and intelligence without virtue can only harm; as the following reasoning proves. No intelligence can take pride in its existence without knowing that it exists; but if, knowing that it exists, it ignores that it does so, not by itself, but by some other, and glorifies itself in itself, not in God, it should consider the words of the Apostle: "What hast thou that thou hast not received? Why dost thou glory as if thou hadst not received it?". He says not merely, "why dost thou glory?" but he adds, "as if thou hadst not received it," showing that it is not blameworthy to glory in having it, but to glory as not having received it. With good reason is such glorying termed vainglory, because it fails to rest upon the solid rock of truth. The Apostle distinguishes this from just glory by saying: "He that glorieth may glory in the Lord, that is in the truth, for God is truth."

We see then that there are two things to know: First, what we are; then, that we are not such of ourselves. If we miss either of these two, we either shall not glory at all, or the glory that we take to ourselves will be "vain." Finally, "if thou know not thyself, go forth and wander after the flocks of thy companions." This is in truth what happens; for when a man in honour knows not his own dignity, he is justly compared, by reason of such ignorance, to the animals that share with him in the corruption and perishing life of this world. Not knowing itself, the creature which reason distinguishes from the beasts confounds itself with them; because, not knowing its own glory, which is all within, it gives way to vain curiosity and occupies itself with external and sensible beauty. It sinks into the likeness of lower creatures by not knowing that it has received a greater thing than they. And this is an ignorance we must sedulously guard against. We must by no means esteem ourselves to be less than God has made us. But with still greater care we must avoid that other ignorance which makes us attribute more to ourselves than we possess; which we do when we mistakenly impute to ourselves the gifts we may be conscious of. Besides these two kinds of ignorance, there remains, to be still more detested and fled from, the presumption which would lead us knowingly to take pride in the good of which we may be conscious, without fear of robbing another of the glory due to Him for things which we well know do not come from ourselves. In the first case, we glory not at all. In the second, we glory, but not in God. In the third, we sin no longer ignorantly but deliberately by usurping that which belongs to God alone. This audacity, compared with the second fault, is greater in this: that it despises God, whereas the other did not know Him. Compared with the first, it assimilates us to devils; whereas the other made us like the beasts. Pride alone, the greatest of all evils, can make us guilty of using the gifts we have received as if they were ours by nature, and of robbing our Benefactor, for our own benefit, of the glory which is His by right. Therefore to excellence and intelligence we must add virtue, their proper fruit. It is by virtue that we seek and attain to the generous Author of all things, Him to whom we ought in all things to render the glory which belongs to Him; otherwise we shall suffer for having known that which was right, and neglected to do it. He that does so has not used His intelligence for good, but "hath devised iniquity on his bed;" he has tried, like a wicked servant, to turn aside and appropriate the glory his good Master should have received, knowing well by the gift of intelligence that he himself had no claim to it. It is clear that excellence without intelligence is useless, and that intelligence without virtue leads to ruin. But, to the man that possesses virtue, neither intelligence nor excellence can be hurtful; he lifts up his voice and praises God eagerly, saying: "Not unto us, O Lord, not unto us, but to Thy name be the glory;" which is to say: "Lord, we lay no claim to intelligence, or excellence; we refer all to Thee, for from Thee we have all that we have."

But we are somewhat wandering, in our desire to prove that they who know not Christ, even they, are sufficiently taught by the natural law, and by the gifts they possess of body and soul, to love God for God's own sake. To repeat in few words what was said above: Where is the infidel who does not know that from Him alone who makes His sun to shine upon the just and unjust, and the rain to fall upon saints and sinners, from Him alone he has received all that is necessary for life; light, air, and food? What man, be he never so impious, refers the excellence peculiar to the human race to any other but to Him who says in Genesis, "Let us make man to Our Own image and likeness"? Who sees the author of intelligence in any but in Him who teacheth all men? From what other hand will any think to receive virtue, but from the God of virtue? God then has good title to be loved for Himself, even on the knowledge of the infidel who is ignorant of Christ; and he that loves not the Lord his God with all his heart and soul and strength is without excuse; for his innate justice and reason cry out from the depth of his soul that he is bound to love Him wholly from whom he holds all things. But it is very difficult, nay, it is impossible by natural strength or the might of free will to refer all to God, instead of keeping back some to our own praise: it is written: "All seek their own;" and elsewhere: "The imagination and thought of man's heart are prone to evil from his youth."

## CHAPTER III

### WHAT MOTIVES CHRISTIANS HAVE, MORE THAN INFIDELS, TO LOVE GOD

BELIEVERS know well the need they have of Jesus crucified; but, whilst they confess and admire His love, they feel no confusion at having so little, nothing but themselves, to return for charity so condescending and so great. Their love is excited by the sense of being so much and so gratuitously loved; for he to whom little love is given, loveth little. Neither Jews nor Pagans feel the pang of love as the Church does, who says: "Stay me up with flowers, compass me about with fruits: because I languish with love." She sees Solomon wearing the diadem with which his mother crowned him. She sees the Only-begotten of the Father staggering under the weight of the cross; the God of all majesty discoloured by blows, covered with spittings; the Author of life and of glory hung upon nails, pierced with a lance and reviled, giving His dear soul for His friends. Gazing on this she feels the sword of love pierce through her heart, and cries out: "Stay me up with flowers, compass me about with fruits, for I languish with love." The pomegranates which the Bride, led into the garden of her Beloved, delights to gather on the tree of life have the taste of the Bread of Heaven and the colour of the Blood of Christ. She sees the deathblow given to death, and its Author swelling the triumph of his Conqueror. She sees the Victor rising gloriously from hell to earth, from earth to heaven, attended by the host of the redeemed; that at "the name of Jesus every knee may bow of those that are in heaven, on earth, and under the earth." Under the ancient curse, the earth was doomed to bring forth thorns and thistles; but the Spouse calls upon it now, restored by divine benediction, to cover her with flowers; and, remembering those words, "My flesh hath flourished again, and with my will I will praise Him," she renews her strength by the fruit of the tree of the cross, and with the flowers of the Resurrection, whose divine perfume attracts the visits of the Beloved. Then he exclaims: "Behold thou art fair, my Beloved, and comely." She shows her desire for His coming, and upon what her hopes are founded; not on her own perfections, but on the sweetness of the flowers gathered in a field that the Lord hath blessed; for they are dear to the Christ who chose to be born and brought up at Nazareth. The heavenly Bridegroom, drawn by the odour, delights to come into the chamber of the heart, when He finds it decked with fruits and perfumed with flowers. He comes with eagerness, and delights to dwell in souls that He sees are devoted to meditation, carefully set on gathering in the fruit of His Passion, and the glorious flowers of His Resurrection. That precious crop which was ripening through the ages of crime and death, and in these last days is fit to be garnered, is the harvest of the fruits of His Passion; but it is in the splendour of the Resurrection that the flowers bloom of the new Springtide which grace has brought upon the earth. In the end of time, at the general resurrection, the abundance of fruit shall be without measure, "for winter is now past, the rain is over and gone, the flowers have appeared in our land." By these words the Bride would say: The summer is come back, with Him who broke up the ice of the old world to restore universal spring, saying: "Behold I make all things new." His body, sown in death, has blossomed in the resurrection, and after His likeness, our plains and valleys, which were dry and bare, or frozen, are new born to life and heat.

The freshness of these flowers, the perfection of the fruits, and the beauty of this garden exhaling such exquisite perfume, are pleasing also to the Father of Him who has made all things new; and, blessing Him, He says: "Behold the smell of my Son is as the smell of a field full of flowers, which the Lord hath blessed;" full of flowers, indeed, for it is of His fulness that we have all received. But the Bride, when she will, may come familiarly and gather flowers and fruit, to dress with them the chamber of her conscience, that the Bridegroom at His coming may find the little bed of her heart giving out the sweetest odours. And in like manner we, if we desire that Christ should come to us and abide in us, must fill our hearts full of the thoughts of His death and resurrection and of faithful recollection of the mercy and the power of which by them He has given us proof. This David meant by the words: "These two things have I heard: that power belongeth to God, and mercy to Thee, O Lord." And Christ has superabundantly proved it; for, having died to expiate our sins, He rose from the dead for our justification, and sent the Holy Spirit for our consolation. Hereafter He will return to consummate our salvation. In His death we have the proof of His mercy, in His resurrection of His power, and of the two united in the rest.

When the Bride entreats to be sustained with aromatic flowers and strengthened with sweet-smelling fruits, it is that she fears lest her love should chill or languish; but she seeks such stimulants only till received into the chamber of her Beloved. She will then feel Him covering her with the kisses she has longed for, and will exclaim: "His left hand is under my head, and His right doth embrace me." She will then feel how far the embrace of the right hand surpasses all sweetness, and that that of the left cannot be compared to it, with which He had caressed her in the first days of His coming. She will understand that "the flesh profiteth nothing; it is the Spirit that quickeneth." She will enter into the sense of His words: "My spirit is above honey, and my inheritance above honey and the honeycomb." If it be also written, "My memory is unto everlasting generations," it is to show that the elect who are not yet satisfied by the presence of the Bridegroom have at least His image for their comfort now whilst time runs on. If it be written, "They shall publish the memory of thine inexhaustible sweetness," it clearly refers to those of whom the Psalmist had before spoken: "Generation and generation shall praise Thy works." On earth there is but the memory of the Bridegroom; in heaven, His perpetual Presence. This is the glory of those who have already arrived in port; and that the consolation of those still buffeting with the waves

## CHAPTER IV

### FOR WHOM THERE IS COMFORT IN THE THOUGHT OF GOD; AND WHO ARE FITTEST TO FEEL LOVE FOR HIM

IT is well to consider who they are that feel comforted by the thought of God. Not those, degraded, who continually vex God, and to whom it is said: "Woe, ye rich, unto you, for you have received your consolation;" but such as can say with truth: "My soul hath refused to be comforted." Well may those who have not yet the joy of the Beloved's presence fix their gaze upon the future; and they who disdain to accept of anything from the stream of passing pleasure, enjoy abundantly, in hope, those joys which shall last for ever. Such are they who seek the face of the Lord, the God of Jacob, and not themselves. The thought of God is sweet to those who sigh after Him, and with every breath recall His presence; but, far from appeasing their hunger for Him, it increases it. This He foretold in the words: "They that eat Me shall yet hunger," and, as if he spake that hungers: "I shall be satisfied when Thy glory shall appear." Yet happy are they even now who hunger and thirst after justice, for only they shall be filled. Woe to you, O perverse, wicked race; woe to you, senseless and besotted people, who do not love the thought of Him, but dread His appearing. Good right ye have to fear, because ye will not now escape from the net of the fowler; for they that will "become rich fall into the snares of the devil." In that day ye shall not fail to fall under the awful, aye and hopeless sentence: "Depart from me, ye cursed, into everlasting fire." But how sweet, how tender is that promise which we hear the Church make every day in remembrance of the Passion: "He that eateth My flesh and drinketh My blood hath everlasting life;" which implies, he that honours My death, and after My example mortifies his flesh upon earth, shall have eternal life; or, if you suffer with Me, you shall also reign with Me. Nevertheless, even to this day, many hearing those words turn and go away sorrowful, saying by their deeds, if not with their lips: "This is a hard saying, who can bear it?" They who, in place of keeping their hearts pure and being faithful to God, love better to set their affections upon uncertain treasures, cannot abide the mention of the Cross; the mere thought of the Passion seems intolerable to them. How will such endure the sentence of the Judge: "Go, ye cursed, into the everlasting fire prepared for the devil and his angels"? These words will crush, like a vast rock, those upon whom they fall. But the Saints shall be blest. Like the Apostle, they have no ambition but to "please God while absent from Him, and still to please Him when they shall be present." They also shall hear their sentence: "Come, ye blessed of my Father, possess the kingdom prepared for you." In that day those who have not kept their hearts aright will, too late, feel how sweet and light is the yoke and burden of Christ, which they proudly refused to bear, through the hardness of their heart, as if it were a vile and crushing weight. It is impossible, poor slaves, to toil for this world's riches, and also to glory in the Cross of our Saviour Jesus Christ; at the same time to desire and labour for earthly things and to taste the sweetness of our Lord. Very fearful you will certainly find Him one day, the thought of whom has never been your joy.

But the believing soul sighs with all her heart after God, and dwells upon the thought of Him; she glories in the disgrace of the Cross, so long as she cannot see her Saviour face to face. She is as the dove of Christ, and she enjoys sleep and rest in the midst of the goods that He has bestowed on her. Her wings are white as silver through the purity and innocence which belong, O Lord Jesus, to the desire of Thine ineffable sweetness; and moreover her hope is that, in the glory reflected from Thy face, her "feathers will shine like gold," and she will overflow with joy and be inundated with light from Thy countenance in the rapture of the Saints. Good reason has she, therefore, to say now with delight: "His left hand is under my head, and His right shall embrace me." His left hand is the memory of that love whose greatness none can ever equal, by which He laid down His life for those whom He loved. His right hand is the beatific vision He has promised to His own, and the content with which He will fill and crown them when they shall enjoy His divine presence. It is written in the Psalms: "At Thy right hand there are delights even to the end." His right hand is therefore justly made the figure of that divine and deifying, that inconceivable felicity which belongs to the vision of God. In like manner the left hand is as the seat of that amazing charity of which I have spoken, of which we can never think too much, for it is upon this hand that the Bride lays her head and rests until this iniquity shall pass away. We may understand her head to mean the intention of her soul, which she leans upon the arm of her Spouse, lest through weakness she might fall away to mere earthly attractions; for the earthly and corruptible burden of the body weighs heavily upon the soul, and drags it down from thoughts to which she cannot fail to rise if she rests upon the contemplation of mercy, to which she had so little claim, love so lavish and so amply proved, gentleness and sweetness so persevering and so exquisite, such unimagined honour. Is it possible that these should not exalt the mind that meditates upon them, detaching it from all unworthy affection, sinking deeper and deeper into it, and making it scorn all which cannot be relished without renouncing these higher enjoyments? Their sweetness, like rare scents, attracts her; she quickens her step blithely, and her heart is all aflame with love. The sense of being loved so tenderly makes her fancy herself cold, though love be her very life. What return is it for a love that comes down from so high, and is so marvellous, if a poor grain of dust be all consumed with gratitude and love? Was not the Majesty of heaven the first to love? Has it not revealed itself as wholly devoted to the work of saving her? For "God so loved the world that He gave His only begotten Son." This is clearly written of God the Father. And again: "He hath delivered His soul to death;" this is said of the Son. And of the Holy Spirit we read: "The Paraclete whom My Father will give you in My name, He will teach you all things, and will bring all things to your remembrance whatsoever I have said unto you." Hereby we see that God loves us, and loves us with His whole being; for the Blessed Trinity altogether loves us, if we dare so to speak of the infinite incomprehensible Being who is one and indivisible.

## CHAPTER V

## OF THE OBLIGATION TO LOVE GOD, ESPECIALLY FOR CHRISTIANS

ALL that has been said proves most clearly the duty of loving God, and His claim upon our love. How is it with the infidel? As he knows not God the Son, so is he also ignorant of the Father and the Holy Spirit; and as he gives no glory to the Son, neither does he glorify the Father who sent Him, nor the Holy Spirit, the gift of both. He knows less of God than we do, therefore it is no wonder he should love Him less. One thing, however, he does know; that to Him who created him, he owes himself entirely. But how will it be with me? for I can plead no ignorance. I know that God made me without any desert of mine, that He satisfies all my wants, comforts me with pity, and governs me with anxious care; and not only so, but I know, besides, that He is my Redeemer, the Author of my eternal salvation, my treasure and my glory. As it is written: "With Him is plentiful redemption;" "By His own blood He entered once into the Holy of Holies, having obtained eternal redemption." He keeps us safe, as it is written: "The Lord knoweth the days of the undefiled, and their inheritance shall be for ever." He enriches us, as He has said: "Good measure, pressed down and shaken together and running over, shall they give into your bosom;" and elsewhere: "The eye hath not seen, O God, what things Thou hast prepared for them that wait for Thee." He fulfils us with glory, as saith the Apostle: "We wait for the Saviour, our Lord Jesus Christ, who will transform our body, now vile and abject, and make it like unto His own, which is full of glory." And again: "The sufferings of this present time are not to be compared to the glory which shall be revealed in us;" and this present time of this world's affliction (so short, so fugitive) produces to us (if only despising the visible we fix our eyes upon things invisible) "an eternal and incomparable weight of glory."

For all of this, what shall I render to the Lord? Both reason and the law of Nature bind me fast to give myself undividedly to Him from whom I hold all that I have, and to devote my entire being to the love of Him. And faith reveals to me that I am constrained to love Him more than myself, the more I understand how I owe to His munificence not only all I am, but moreover the gift of Himself. But let us consider that, ere yet the day of Christian faith had come, before God had put on our flesh and died upon a cross, gone down into hell and ascended to the Father, that is, before the fulness of His love for us had shone forth, long before, man had been commanded to love the Lord his God with all his heart, with all his soul, with all his strength, that is, with his whole being, with all the love of which he is capable, as a creature endowed with intelligence and will. Could it be unjust of God to claim for Himself His own work and His gifts? Why should not the work love God who made it, having also received the power to love; and why not love Him with all its powers, if it be only by God that it possesses any? Consider, too, that man has not only been called into being out of nothing, without any anterior claim, but also that he has been so called to be raised to high dignity. We shall thus see more clearly our obligation to love Him wholly, and His right to our love. Moreover, when man had sunk to the level of the beasts that perish, did God not intervene to reinstate and save him? Is not this the marvel of His goodness and His mercy? For by sin we had fallen from the dignity of our creation, to become imbruted like the ox that eateth grass and hath not the light of reason. If I owe my whole self to my Creator, what do I not owe to my Redeemer, and to such a Redeemer! It was a far less work to create, than to redeem; for God had but to speak the word and all things were made; but to repair the fall of that, which one word had created, what wonders had He not to perform, what cruelties, nay, what humiliations, had He not to suffer!

What, therefore, shall I render to the Lord for all that He hath done for me! By creating, He gave me to myself; but He restored me to myself when He gave Himself to me: first given and then restored, I doubly owe myself to Him. But, what do I owe to God for the gift of Himself? If I gave Him my whole being a thousand times over, what would that be in comparison of God?

## CHAPTER VI

### A SUMMARY OF WHAT HAS HITHERTO BEEN SAID

CONFESS that God deserves to be greatly loved, or rather that He should be loved beyond measure. He was the first to love; He so great, we so little; He loves us to excess, just as we are, and without any claim whatsoever on our side. This is why the rightful measure of our love to God is to exceed all measure; for God, the object of our love, being infinite, how can we weigh or measure what we owe to Him in love? Moreover, our love is not a free offering; it is the payment of a debt. And, besides, as it is the I Am, eternal and immense, the Divine Love, God, whose greatness has no limits nor His wisdom bounds, who is the "Peace which passeth all understanding;" as, I say, it is such a God who loves us, is it possible for us to say we will love Him so much and no more? "I will love Thee, O Lord, my strength and my defence, my refuge and my salvation," who art to me all that my soul needs, and all that my heart desires. My God and my Help, I will love Thee with all my strength; not according to what Thou deservest, but according to my little capacity. I will love Thee more when Thou hast given me more power of loving; but never, never as Thou shouldst be loved. Thine eyes see my foolishness, my inability; but I know that Thou writest in Thy book those who do what they can, even when they cannot do what they ought. Have I not said enough to prove how God should be loved, and by what gifts He has merited our love? I merely name His gifts, because the excellence of them who can express, who can understand, who can feel?

## CHAPTER VII

### THE REWARDS AND ADVANTAGE OF THE LOVE OF GOD. THE HEART OF MAN IS NOT TO BE SATISFIED BY EARTHLY THINGS

LET us see what benefit accrues to us from loving God. Though we may see this ever so imperfectly, that is better than to be blind to it. We have spoken (though in a manner unworthy of God, yet to the best of our power) of God's right to our love; we will now speak of the recompense He has attached to our loving Him; for whilst we must love God, independently of all reward, we shall none the less be rewarded for having loved Him. True charity cannot be left without salary, although she is not mercenary and seeketh not her own. Love is a going forth of the soul, not a contract; it is not the result of a convention, and is not to be acquired by agreement; it is spontaneous in its impulses, and likens us to itself; also true love is its own satisfaction. Its recompense lies in the object of its love; for whatever be that which we seem to love, if our real object be something else, it is really that something which we love, and not that by which our heart strives to attain it. St. Paul preached not the gospel for his daily bread, but the bread which kept him alive enabled him to preach the gospel. What he loved was the gospel, not the bread. True love seeks no reward, but it merits one; it is very certain that no one proposes to pay for love, although it not only deserves its recompense, but shall surely have it. In a lower class of things, who are they that are excited by the offer of rewards? Those that are slack and unloving. Does it ever occur to any one to persuade with pay those that are burning to be allowed to serve? One does not give money to a starving man to engage him to eat, no more than to a tender mother to induce her to give suck to her child, to get a vinedresser to protect his vines, or a householder to rebuild his fallen house. Far less does he who loves God need to be urged by the promise of a recompense which is other than God Himself; otherwise it would be the reward he loved, not God.

It is natural to a reasonable being to desire that which appears to him, according to his particular mode of thinking, better than what he possesses; and never to be satisfied if a good thing wants the particular quality which he prefers. If he loves beauty he will desire what seems to him most beautiful. If he plumes himself on the possession of a very precious jewel, he will desire to possess a still more splendid one; and whatever riches he may have, his nature is to want more. Is it not a thing we see every day, the owner of immense property and wealth buying up more land, and never content but in extending his estates? Those who dwell in vast palaces, are they not for ever building new ones, always altering, making round the cornered, and the cornered round? Are not men in high position constantly aspiring to higher, constantly striving to rise, out of an ambition more and more difficult to appease? There is no limit to such restlessness, because, in all such things, it is impossible to reach a point absolutely good and high. But it is not astonishing that so long as a man can see beyond him something greater and more perfect, he should be dissatisfied with his own possession of what is less and worse. What does seem foolish beyond all expression is, always to be longing for things which cannot even lull to sleep our desires, far less satisfy them. What follows? this—that the heart, tempted by many deceitful charms, wearies itself to no purpose, is always craving, and counts for nothing what it has enjoyed, compared to what it fain would have; and is tormented, by desire of what it has not, out of all delight with what it possesses. All one cannot have; for the little it is possible to get, the price of labour must be paid; and it must be enjoyed with trembling; nay, with the miserable certainty that one day it must be lost, though the date of that day be not known.

I have described the conduct of a perverted will blindly seeking the sovereign good. It makes haste in vain, the plaything of its own vanity, deceived by iniquity. Why wear out the day in fruitless struggle this way and that, and be caught by death unsatisfied? In such toils do the profane entangle themselves who seek about, like fools, to obtain their souls' desires. They consume their life in useless efforts and arrive at no perfect happiness; for they are in love with created things, not with the Creator, and they try them, one and then another, before they dream of trying the Lord that made them all. Yet, if they could have their hearts' desire and achieve the possession of the world, less Him who is its author, they would feel at last, by the same law which has ruled their life, that Him they must have, or never rest. They have gone from one ambition to another, coveting always some better thing; and now, masters of all in heaven and earth, they would soon find all insufficient, and discover that they were forced to seek Him who is wanting still, they must seek God Himself. Once discover that, once attain unto Him, there is peace; it is impossible to go beyond. The soul must cry out: "It is good for me to adhere to my God;" or, "What besides Thee have I in heaven, and besides Thee what do I desire upon earth?" and again: "Thou art the God of my heart, and the God that is my portion for ever." Even this way would a soul necessarily end in God if it could try in sequence all lesser things than He.

But life is too short, and strength would fail for any such attempt; also the number of competitors is too great. It would be impossible to try all creatures and find them wanting. It were more easy and more advantageous to do the work in imagination than in reality. Our minds have been endowed with more activity and perspicacity than our hearts precisely for this end—that they may go first and prevent the heart from attaching itself to what the mind has not first found desirable. "Prove all things: hold fast that which is good." The first should prepare the ground for the second, so that the heart should follow the judgment of the mind. Otherwise there is no hope of "ascending into the mountain of the Lord, and dwelling in His holy place;" and it is in vain that we possess a reasoning mind, if we do as the beasts do, and only obey our senses, the reason not interfering. They who are not guided by reason, run indeed in the race, but they run without chance of winning. How should they win, seeing they care not first for the prize, but put that last of all? How should they do other than entangle themselves in a maze without beginning or end? Not so with the just. Warned by the blame addressed to those who thus err (for the way is wide and well trodden that leads to death), they choose the royal road which turns to neither right nor left, for "the path of the just is straight." They take the shortest road, guided by a word as simple as simplifying, commanding them not to heed what their eyes may see, but to sell all and give to the poor; for blessed indeed are such poor, and the kingdom of heaven is theirs. The Lord knoweth the way of the just, and commendeth it. He knoweth also the way of the sinner, in which he cannot but perish. The just are happy in their poverty, and the rich unsatisfied in their abundance; for the wise man saith: "He that loveth riches shall reap no fruit from them." But they who "hunger and thirst after justice shall be filled." Justice is their needful food. As to the things of this world, the soul is no more nourished by them than the body is by air. If we were to see a starving man inhaling with wide open mouth, drinking long draughts of wind to quench his thirst, we should say, Poor fool! So is it with those who seek to satisfy the soul with worldly goods, which do but puff it out as with wind, and no more feed it than things spiritual feed our bodies. "Bless the Lord, O my soul, who satisfieth thy desire with good things." He filleth thee out of His fulness; at once giving thee thy desire, and exciting thee to wish for more. He prevents, He sustains, He fills thee; He kindles desire in thy heart, and He Himself is the Object of all desire.

I have said that the motive of our love to God is God Himself, and it is well said, for He is both the efficient cause and the final end of our love. He is such that it is impossible to know and not to love Him; not also to hope in Him; for, if we did not hope to love Him perfectly hereafter, our present love for Him would be nothing. Our love is prepared and recompensed by His. He first loves us out of His exceeding goodness; then He claims the due return of love, and permits us in the future the most glorious hopes. He is generous to those who call upon Him, but He can give nothing better than Himself. He Himself is the end of our merits, and our reward. He is the food of holy souls, the ransom of those that are yet in captivity. If the Lord be good to the soul that seeketh Him, what is He to that soul which hath found Him? But this may seem strange, that no one can seek the Lord who hath not already found Him; for His will is to be found that He may be yet more sought; and sought, that He may be more entirely found. But, though He may be sought and found, He can never be forestalled. He is always first; and if we say: "In the morning my prayer shall prevent Thee," it is nevertheless quite certain that that prayer would be very chilly if, O God, thine inspiration did not precede it.

We have spoken of the consummation of the love of God, let us now see what are its beginnings.

## CHAPTER VIII

### WE BEGIN BY THE LOVE OF SELF, THIS BEING FOR US THE FIRST DEGREE OF LOVE

LOVE is one of the four natural affections that all the world knows, and which need not be enumerated. Now, it is but natural and right first of all to love the Author of nature; and the first commandment, which is the greatest, is: "Thou shalt love the Lord thy God." But nature is too soft and weak for such a precept; she must begin by loving herself; this is the love which is called carnal, with which man loves himself first and above all; as it is written: "That is not first which is spiritual, but that which is natural." We love first by nature, not by precept—"No man ever hated his own flesh." But if this love should increase too much; if like a river between banks it overflow and flood the lands about, it then becomes voluptuousness, and this dyke is opposed to it: "Thou shalt love thy neighbour as thyself." Justly may he that shares our nature share our love. Wherefore, if any one cannot so love his brethren as to think of their wants, or let us even say of their pleasures, let him deny himself in those very things, in order that he may learn. Let a man think of himself as much as ever he will, if only he take care to think equally of his neighbour. Such, O man, is the curb and just limit imposed upon thee by the law of thy being and by thy conscience, that thou be not carried away by thy selfishness to thy destruction, leaving thy nature at the mercy of the enemies of thy soul; that is, of thy passions. It is far better that thou go shares with thy neighbours than with thy enemies; and if, as the wise man advises, man renounces his passions, contents himself with food and raiment, and is willing to moderate his love for those things of the flesh which war against the spirit, he will, I think, find small difficulty in giving to his neighbour what he refuses to the enemy of his soul. His love will be contained within the bounds of justice and moderation, from the moment that he consecrates to his brethren that which he refuses to himself. Selfishness becomes benevolence by taking a wider range.

But if through imparting to our neighbour we bring ourselves to want? What is our remedy? Prayer. We have only to pray with confidence to Him who giveth all things liberally and upbraideth not; who "openeth His hand and filleth with blessing every living creature;" for we cannot doubt that He who giveth to most men more than they need, will willingly give to him who prays for what is indispensable; for it is written: "Seek first the kingdom of God, and His justice, and all these things shall be added unto you." God hereby binds Himself to provide what is essential for him that denies himself and loves his neighbour; for to put on the yoke of purity and sobriety rather than be the slave of our passions, this is to seek first the kingdom of God and to implore His help against the tyranny of sin; and it is justice to share our natural blessings with those that share our nature.

But in order that love for our neighbour be entirely right, God must have His part in it; it is not possible to love our neighbour as we ought to do, except in God. Now he that loves not God can love nothing in Him. We must therefore begin by loving God, and so love our neighbour in Him. God is the author, as of all other things, so of our love for Him—and more—as He created nature, so He sustains it; for she could neither exist nor subsist without Him. That we might thoroughly know this, and not attribute anything to ourselves, God, in the depths of His wisdom and love, made us subject to tribulation. Being feeble and needy, we are forced to turn to God, and being saved by Him we render glory to His name. These are His own words: "Call upon Me in the day of trouble; I will deliver thee, and thou shalt glorify Me." In this way man, by nature animal and carnal, with no love but for himself, is brought through self-love to love God, realising that all his ability, at any rate for good, he has from God, and without Him is able to do nothing.

## CHAPTER IX

## OF THE SECOND AND THIRD DEGREES OF LOVE

FIRST, then, man has some love for God for his own sake, not for God's. It is already something to feel the limits of his own capacity, to know what he cannot do without the help of God, and to keep right with Him who sustains his life and strength. But, let a train of disasters befall and oblige him perpetually to have recourse to God, if he still get the aid he wants, his heart must be of brass or marble not at last to be touched by the goodness of his helper, not to begin at length to love Him for Himself. Let the frequency of trials bring us often to the feet of God, surely it is impossible, but we must begin to know Him, and, knowing Him, must come to discern His sweetness. It soon follows that we are brought to love Him rightly, far more for the sweetness and beauty that we find in Him than for our own self-interest. In the words of the Samaritans to the woman: "We now believe, not for thy saying; for we ourselves have heard Him, and know that this is indeed the Saviour of the world." In like manner, we come to say to our natural self: It is not because of thee that we love the Lord, but we have tasted ourselves, and found how sweet He is. The necessities of this life are a kind of language proclaiming in transports of joy and thanksgiving the blessings of which they have taught us the value. When this has once been learnt, it is easy enough to obey the precept and love our neighbour as ourself; for, if we love God truly, we love all that is His, and it is henceforth easy to submit to the precept: "Purify your hearts in the obedience of charity, with a brotherly love." We are bound to fulfil willingly so just a command, a command, moreover, so full of profit because it is disinterested. It is a love most pure, for it is shown simply in holy deeds and truth; most just, for it returns that which it receives. Whoso loves with this love, loves as he is loved, and seeks no more his own, but the things of Jesus Christ, even as Jesus Christ has sought us. Herein we see such love as that which said, "Give praise to the Lord, for He is good." He that loves God because He is good, not to him, but in Himself, loves God indeed for God, and not as he does of whom the Scripture saith: "He will praise Thee when Thou shalt do well to him."

## CHAPTER X

## THE FOURTH DEGREE OF LOVE IS TO LOVE SELF ONLY FOR GOD

HAPPY is he who can rise to the fourth degree of love, and loves himself only for God's sake. "Thy justice, O Lord, is as the high mountains." It is even so of this fourth degree of love, "a great mountain in which God is well pleased to dwell." "Who shall ascend into the mountain of the Lord?" "Who will give me wings like a dove, and I will fly thither and be at rest?" "His place is in peace, and his abode in Zion." "Woe is me that my sojourning is prolonged." When shall this flesh and blood, this dust and mire of which I am made, be able to go up there? When shall this soul of mine, entranced with love for God, look on herself as broken sherds, yearn after God, and lose herself in Him, for "He who is joined to the Lord is one spirit"? When shall she cry out: "My flesh and my heart have fainted away; Thou art the God of my heart, and the God that is my portion for ever"? Holy and happy is he who but once, for but one moment, has felt something like this in his mortal life; for this is no human happiness, it is life eternal so to lose oneself, as if one were empty of self, as if one were not. If some poor mortal attains to this, for one moment and as it were unawares, this evil time seems begrudgingly to delay and embitter his joy. This body of death drags him down, the cares and anxieties of life pull him back, the corruption of the flesh refuses its support, and his duty to his neighbour calls on him loudly to come down, and cry out: "Lord, I suffer violence, answer Thou for me;" or thus: "Unhappy man that I am, who shall deliver me from the body of this death?"

We read in Holy Scripture that God hath made all things for Himself. His creatures are therefore bound to conform themselves, at least in some measure, to the mind of their Maker. We ought to offer ourselves entirely to Him, studying only His good pleasure, not our own. We shall find happiness, much less in seeking our own advantage, than in the accomplishment of His will in us, according as we daily pray: "Thy will be done on earth as it is in Heaven." O pure and holy love! most sweet and blessed affection! O complete submission of a disinterested soul; most perfect in that there is no thought of self; most sweet and tender in that the soul's whole feeling is divine! To attain to this, is for the soul to be deified; as a small drop of water appears lost if mixed with wine, taking its taste and colour; and as, when plunged into a furnace, a bar of iron seems to lose its nature and assume that of fire; or as the air filled with the sun's beams seems rather to become light than to be illuminated. So it is with the natural life of the Saints; they seem to melt and pass away into the will of God. For if anything merely human remained in man, how then should God be all in all? It is not that human nature will be destroyed, but that it will attain another beauty, a higher power and glory. When shall that be? To whom shall it be given to see and know it? When shall I come and appear before the face of God? O God, my Lord, my heart hath said to Thee: "My face hath sought Thee; Thy face, O Lord, will I seek." Will it be given to such as I to see Thy holy temple?

In this life, the heart is obliged to take some thought of the body, the mind to see that its health and powers are kept unimpaired; and I think that it is impossible, so long as our energies are thus divided, to rest wholly in God and in the contemplation of Him, impossible perfectly to obey the precept, "Thou shalt love the Lord thy God with all thy heart, with all thy soul, and with all thy strength." We may not hope to possess the fourth degree of love, or rather to be possessed by it, until we have put on a body spiritual and immortal, pure and calm, obedient and subject in all to the spirit, which cannot be our doing, but only the work of the power of God in favour of such as please Him. Our soul will easily attain to this perfect love when neither the burden nor the temptations of this body oppress her; then she will spring untrammelled to her joy in the Lord. But are we to doubt that the souls of the holy martyrs before quitting their triumphant bodies tasted, at least in some small measure, of this happiness? This we know for certain, that immense love filled and enraptured their souls, to give them strength to lay down their lives and to endure the torments which they suffered. Still the joy of their triumph must have been thereby abated.

## CHAPTER XI

## THE SAINTS WILL HAVE PERFECT LOVE ONLY AFTER THE GENERAL RESURRECTION

WHAT may we then believe of souls already freed from the burden of the flesh? I believe them to be altogether immersed in the fathomless depths of eternal light, and of a luminous eternity. But if, as we may not deny, they still desire and hope to rejoin the bodies they formerly inhabited, it is clear that they are not altogether changed, but that still their bodies claim some part in them, although it may be very small. And, until death be wholly swallowed up in victory, until the glory of eternity shall have pervaded every corner of the domain of night, and the clarity of celestial light shine even in our bodies, until then our souls can never cast themselves into God, and wholly give themselves to Him. Until then the chains of the body still impede them, be it only by a natural affection which they have neither the will nor the power to forsake; and, till the restitution of our bodies, our souls can never be swallowed up in God, which is their absolute perfection. If the union with Him could be consummated by the soul alone, she would no more desire the body; but when the soul leaves the body, it is gain, and greater gain when it rejoins it. Finally, "precious in the sight of the Lord is the death of His saints." If death can be so praised, how shall it be with life? that life! The soul may well think to obtain increase of glory from its body, because, though infirm and mortal, it has contributed greatly to its merits. To "them that love God all things work together unto good;" and the soul which loves God profits by its poor, weak body, whether living, dead, or risen—living, by bringing forth with her fruits of penance; dead, by resting from its labour; risen, the two together attain the consummation of all joy. It is clear then that without the body the soul is not perfected; as in every state it is essential to her good.

The body then is for the soul a faithful companion; if it be a burden, it is also a help; when it ceases to aid, it also ceases to hinder; when again it helps, it is no more a burden. The first state is laborious, but profitable; the second inactive, but in no sense tedious; and the third is glorious. Hear how the Bridegroom in the Canticles invites the soul to these three conditions: "Eat, O friends, and drink, and be inebriated, my dearly beloved." The souls whom He invites to eat are those still toiling in their bodies; those that are at rest in death, He presses to drink; those who are once more clothed upon to be inebriated; and, calling these His dearly beloved, He implies that they are filled with charity: for to the first He saith only "friends;" for they who still toil under the weight of the body are dear to Him according to the love they bear.

Those who are delivered from the burden of the flesh are dearer yet, because of the freedom and fulness their love has acquired. But, compared with all these, most dearly beloved are they who, clothed again in the robe of the glorious body, are transported with the love of God in joyful liberty from everything which might draw them down or hinder their upward flight. Not till thus perfected are they so delivered, for in the first case the body wearies the spirit and keeps it back; in the second, the body is an object of hope and of personal desire, which has in it the taint of self. The faithful soul begins by eating bread, but, alas, "in the sweat of her face;" for so long as she is in the body she does but walk by faith, which should work by love, for faith without works is dead. Now these are the works which are her bread, according to the word of the Lord: "My bread is to do the will of my Father." When she has put off the body of death she ceases to eat the bread of sorrow, and, as at the close of a meal, she drinks long draughts of the wine of love; but this wine is not yet unmixed, for, as saith the Bridegroom in the Canticles, "I have drunk my wine with my milk," for with the wine of God's love the soul mixes milk; namely the desire of re-union with her body which she loves with the softness of natural affection. Already she feels the strength of the divine love which she drinks, but it does not yet transport her; the mingling of milk still tempers it. Inebriation troubles the spirit so that it forgets itself; but that is not the state of the soul still yearning for its body, which is yet to rise. She does not wholly lose the sense of self. But when she has regained this only thing that lacks, what hinders that she should altogether cast herself into God, losing even her own likeness, in being made like unto Him? No obstacle remaining, she can lift to her lips the cup of wisdom of which it is written: "My chalice which inebriateth me, how goodly is it;" and who can wonder that she is transported with the abundance that fills the house of God; free from all care, she drinks, in the Kingdom of the Father, long, tranquil draughts of the wine of the Son, pure and new.

It is wisdom that gives this threefold banquet, where all the food is charity. She gives bread to those who have still to labour, wine for those to drink who already enjoy rest; and inebriates those who are gone into the kingdom of heaven. When her guests have eaten, she serves to them wine. So long as we toil in this life, bearing on us a mortal body, we must eat of the bread our labour has found us, we must eat laboriously and swallow it; but, scarce have we breathed our last sigh, when we begin to drink in our spiritual life, receiving the cup, and drinking in happy restfulness. When all is accomplished, and the body is risen to life and restored to the soul, they drink to inebriation of the chalice that never fails. This is the meaning of those words: "Eat, O my friends, and drink; and be inebriated, my dearly beloved." In this life, eat; after death you shall drink; in the kingdom of the resurrection you shall be inebriated; you whom I well may call my dearly beloved. Are they not truly so who are admitted to the marriage feast of the Lamb, who sit at His table, eating and drinking in His kingdom, when "He presents to Himself a glorious church, not having spot or wrinkle, or any such thing"? It is then He will inebriate His dearly beloved, pouring out to them a "torrent of delights;" for when the Bridegroom shall clasp the Bride in His loving and chaste embrace, a torrent of delight shall rejoice the City of God, which I hold to mean no other than the Son of God, who, "passing, will minister unto them that sit at meat." So He hath promised that the just may feast, and rejoice before God, and be delighted with gladness. From thence comes satiety which is never satisfied; ardour which is insatiable, yet most calm and peaceful; the eternal and incomparable desire to possess, which arises from no want; that inebriation without excess, which comes from the enjoyment, not of wine, but of God and His Truth. The soul hath reached for ever the fourth degree of love, when she loves only God, and loves Him supremely; when she loves for no gain, for Himself alone; so that He is her reward, the eternal recompense of those who love Him, and shall love Him for ever.

# FRAGMENTS FROM A FRAGMENT BY ST. BERNARD HIS LAST WORK FRAGMENTS

THERE are in Holy Scripture many songs of praise; but only one is styled the Canticle of canticles. Moses, Israel, Deborah, Judith, and many others, sang a song to the Lord to glorify Him for wonders received at His hands; but only Solomon, the wise and pacific king (crowned with glory and goods and blessings, living in perfect peace, in no need of the gifts and deliverances for which others gave thanks), only he sang, by the inspiration of the Holy Ghost, the glory of Jesus Christ and of the Church, in their mystical, eternal espousals; an Epithalamium celebrating the aspirations of a holy soul, and the transports of a purely spiritual joy, to the glory of Him who is the King of kings, and Lord of lords; for whose sake, as He is above all, and His praise most excellent, the Song of Solomon is called the Canticle of canticles.

It is the perfection of all other praises, and only the grace of God can teach its meaning, for it can only be learned by experience. Let those who have it not burn with desire to obtain it. It is not a hymn of the lips, but an outburst of the heart. It is not a harmony of voices, but a concord of wills. It is only to be understood within, not heard without. And only they two have to do with it, the Bridegroom and the Bride; for it is a nuptial hymn expressing the purity and closeness of spiritual embraces, perfect union of will, perfect mutual oneness of affection and inclination.

When I think of the eager yearning with which the patriarchs and ancient servants of God sighed for the Incarnation of our Lord Jesus Christ, I grieve and weep for my own insensibility, and for the indifference of the age we live in. Who of us feels a joy that He has come equal to the longing which they felt for the fulfilment of His promise?

The opening words of the Canticle: "Let Him kiss me with the kiss of His mouth," express the holy impatience of those men; as if they said, "What is to me Moses? he hath stammering lips; Isaiah's are impure; Jeremiah is but a child; let him speak to me no more through them; they are but a cloud; let

Him kiss me with the kiss of His mouth; let His presence, His teaching, be to me as a spring of water welling up into eternal light. Not that I presume to ask Him to kiss me with His mouth; that privilege is not for me; that happiness, all singular and sacred, belongs to the Word of God alone; to that humanity which He assumed in His incarnation." When the Godhead of the Word was united to a body, that union was the kiss once only given by God and once received by man; for Jesus is the mediator between God and man. In Him the union of two natures brings together things divine and human. It marries heaven and earth in perfect peace. No Saint has ever dared to say: Let Him kiss me with His mouth; for that kiss is Jesus Christ, our peace, who of two hath made but one; the Man, who, being God, reigns for ever with the Father and the Holy Ghost.

I would fain know if any one of you has received grace to say: Let Him kiss me with the kiss of His mouth. It belongs not to many so to speak, but he who once has been so honoured is perpetually excited to desire it again, and passionately pressed to ask for it. None can imagine who has not felt it; it is a hidden manna for which he that hath eaten shall still hunger; it is a fountain sealed, of which whoso drinks shall still thirst. Hear him speak who had tasted: "Give me again the joy of the Saviour." But a soul borne down by sin, subject to the frailties of the flesh, which has never tasted the sweetness of the Holy Spirit, such an one aspires to no such grace. I will tell you where such may well abide: behind the feet of the Divine Saviour, his eyes on the ground, like the Publican not daring to look up to heaven, lest venturing to gaze upon glory he be blinded by excess of light. Think it not beneath you to stand where the woman stood who "was a sinner." After the example of that most blessed penitent, kneel at His feet, prostrate yourself like her, you that are miserable, that you may cease to be so. Kiss His feet, so to appease His wrath; wash them with tears, not for their cleansing, but for your own; and venture not to lift your eyes until you also hear those words: "Your sins are forgiven."—"Arise, arise, daughter of Sion; arise, you that are captive, and lie no more in the dust." But not yet must you presume to think of the kiss of His mouth. If you obtain His hand to kiss, be more than satisfied; for if Jesus Himself said to me: "Thy sins are forgiven thee," what would that avail if I could not thenceforth keep from sin? What profits it to wash my feet if I soil them again? I have long been sunk in the mire: if I fall back again now, my last state will be worse than my first. He who healed me said: "Now go and sin no more lest a worse thing come unto thee." My safety is in His hands. He who gave me heart to repent, He also must bestow on me strength to abstain from sin. Woe to me if, even while I do penance, He were to withdraw His hand, for without Him I can do nothing, absolutely nothing. I can neither repent, nor keep myself from sin. I hear the counsel of the Wise Man: "Ask not twice the same grace," and I shudder when I think of the sentence of the Judge cursing the tree that brought not forth fruit. I need another grace by which, having repented of my sins, I may have heart to bring forth worthy fruits of penance, that I may not fall back into my first misery. This I must obtain before I presume to look up and sue for a royal favour. The presumption of a sinner is hateful unto God, but the shame of a penitent is very dear to Him. What! defiled with the filth of sin, could I so much as think of touching His sacred lips? No; but ask that He may reach out His hand to you to kiss; that that hand may lift you up and wash away your impurities. Lift you up! and how? By enabling you to aspire to higher favours, encouraging you to bring forth worthy fruits of heartfelt penitence which are the works of piety. By these graces He will lift you up from the dunghill, giving you the hope of yet better things; and, when He gives His gifts, kiss His hand; give to Him all the glory; offer Him a double sacrifice in that He hath first forgiven your sins, and then bestowed His graces on you. It may be then that you will have courage to go on to something holier still, for as you grow in grace you will grow in trust, your love will intensify, you will ask the more fervently as you will more keenly feel your need, and to him that asks God gives liberally. I think He will not even refuse you that kiss, the most excellent and sacred of all, containing in itself the sweetness of ineffable consolation. By that most holy kiss we are united with Him, and through His infinite goodness we become one spirit with Him.

"Let Him kiss me with the kiss of His mouth." Who speaks? The Bride. And who is she? She is the soul that is athirst for God.

Let us consider the dispositions of various classes. Slaves dread the face of their masters. Mercenaries care only for their pay. Disciples wait upon the words of their teacher. Sons honour their fathers. But one who asks only for a kiss is aflame with love. There is nothing in all Nature that surpasses such love, above all when it is fixed upon its fountain, God. The love of God and of the soul can be expressed in no way so perfectly as by the mutual love of Bride and Bridegroom, all being in common between them, and neither having any separate possessions. For his wife, the man must leave father and mother, for that he and she are one flesh; and the woman must forget her people and her father's house, that her husband may delight in her beauty. Since this relation is the ideal one of love, it is well that the name of Bride should be given to the soul that loves. The loving soul asks a kiss; not freedom, rest, reward; not knowledge; nor yet riches; only this, a kiss. She asks it as a modest bride, warm with a holy love, and needing not to disguise her affection. Having a great favour to ask as from a king, she makes no excuse, or preface; she goes straight to her point, and, speaking confidently out of the abundance of her heart, she simply says: "Let Him kiss me with the kiss of His mouth;" as if she said: "What is there in heaven or earth that I desire in comparison with Thee?" She is chaste, for she cares for nothing else but Him; she is pure, for all her desire is spiritual. She is eager in her love, for she forgets even the majesty of Him to whom she speaks; for of whom does she ask this favour? Of Him who, with one look, makes all the earth to tremble. But it is written: "Perfect love casteth out fear."

To return to what I said before. In these words, "No man knoweth the Father but the Son, and he to whom the Son will reveal Him," a kiss is spoken of, a kiss ineffable, which no creature had ever yet received. The Father loves the Son, and embraces Him with a love like to none other. The Most High embraces His Equal; the Eternal, His Co-Eternal; the only God, His only Son.

Hear also of another kiss: He breathed on them and said, "Receive the Holy Ghost." Was it material breath He breathed? Oh, no. It was the invisible Spirit which was given by this breath of the Lord, that all might know that He proceedeth equally from the Son and the Father; a kiss equally His who gives and who receives. The kiss of His mouth also suffices to the Bride, because that kiss is the infusion of the Holy Spirit, the unalterable Peace, the indissoluble Link, the invisible Love and Unity of the Father and the Son. The Bride, inspired by the Holy Ghost, is bold to ask to receive Him. She is bold, because the words of our Lord encourage her: "None knoweth the Son but the Father, and none knoweth the Father but the Son, or him to whom it pleaseth the Son to reveal Him." Now, to know the Father and the Son, their goodness must needs be known, and that goodness is the Holy Ghost.

When then the Bride asks a kiss, she asks for this: the triple knowledge of the Father, of the Son, and of the Holy Spirit; and this revelation is by the Holy Ghost who enlightens the understanding to know, and also kindles the will to love; or, in the words of St. Paul: "The love of God is shed abroad in our hearts by the Holy Ghost whom He hath given us." O holy soul, recollect thyself in deepest reverence, for He is the Lord thy God!

It requires indeed discretion to give honour acceptably to a king; but strong love overleaps discretion. The Bride breathes forth the heaviness of her heart. It is not presumption, nor that she lacks humility. She is sunk in sadness, she is like earth without water, she is heavy-hearted, and her spirit is oppressed within her; she has struggled on in the sweat of her brow, languid and weary. Are there not many souls that complain of such dulness and dreariness? And is not the very thing they want what the Bride sighs for here: "Let Him kiss me with the kiss of His mouth"? They languish for the spirit of wisdom and knowledge; for knowledge to understand, for wisdom to taste what they know.

She spoke of the Bridegroom and He appeared. He grants her prayer, and gives her the boon she besought, as it is written: "Thou hast given the desire of the heart, and hast not denied the request of the lips." Of those who wait upon the Lord in prayer, very many will bear witness how often this is so. Cold and dry, they persevere; and, of a sudden, grace is vouchsafed them; they are conscious of an inundation as it were of piety; love and sweetness and delight overflow; they are full and able to give forth abundantly to those in need of the sweetness of God's consolations. Forthwith the soul breaks forth in praise of Him who hath done such great things for her, and accounts for her boldness by extolling the perfections of her Spouse on which her trust was founded. These are His patience with sinners and His clemency to penitents; a double sweetness. So David says: "The Lord is long suffering, and plenteous in mercy;" and St. Paul: "Despisest thou the riches of His goodness and patience and long-suffering? Knowest thou not that the benignity of God leadeth thee to penance?" And of His facility for pardoning it is written: "Let the wicked forsake his sins and the unjust man his thoughts, and let him return unto the Lord and He will have mercy, and to our God and He will abundantly pardon." "For these perfections of which I have long since tasted, for no worthiness in myself, I had confidence to ask Thee what my soul desired." So speaks the Spouse, and what is true of the Lord is also true of His servants, and especially of those that have to teach. If they suffer not with the suffering, and rejoice not in their relief and benediction, they are useless to others and worse than useless to themselves. Consider how it is with a holy Pastor. Like a mother among her little ones, he dispenses to each of his children according to their need: to the weak the milk of babes; to the tempted, most sweet sympathy and counsel; is any timid and faint-hearted; how he will encourage, and praise, and find ingenious points of consolation! Or if any be gay, and lively, making rapid progress, how he will in his delight give him wise counsels, animate him to further efforts, and assist him to persevere, and every day to go forward, on and on. Such a Pastor is all to all, conforming himself to each, feeling in his own heart the feelings and disposition of each one, no less devoted to those that falter, than to those who steadily advance. Alas, for such as seek their own! If this be true of any who have undertaken the charge of souls, their evil heart is as a foundry in which are made the scourges, nails and lance, the cross and death of Jesus Christ.

There are other qualities of the Bride, the Church, and of every holy soul, which we may call perfumes. They too have their beginning and perfection in our Lord. We will treat of three: the perfume of contrition; the perfume of devotion; and the perfume of piety. The first gives pain and pierces; the second soothes and cheers; the third drives away and cures all evil. Let us discourse of each minutely.

First, then, the perfume which the soul composes, when it begins to examine its conduct, heaps together all its sins of whatever kind, and putting them into the cauldron of conscience distils them, as it were, over the fire of grief and repentance. This is the first perfume of the sinful soul; and while she has no better to present, this, though composed of such vile materials, she should faithfully persevere in offering; for God will never scorn a humble and contrite heart. The more conscious a soul is of her misery, the less will God reproach her. Dare we call it so vile however? Is it not that with which the sinful woman anointed the feet of Jesus, and the Gospel says, "The whole house was filled with the odour of the ointment"? The open, thorough repentance of a sinner perfumes the whole Church; it is "a savour of life unto life," so sweet and penetrating that it reaches even to the abode of the blessed; and "the Truth" Himself hath said: "There is joy in the presence of the angels of God over one sinner that repenteth." Be full of gladness then, poor penitent, and in preparing this acceptable ointment, begrudge not the myrrh and its bitterness; God will be gracious to the remorse of a penitent heart.

The second perfume is more precious in that it is made of things more valuable. We have no need to go forth for the materials of the first, they exist abundantly within us; but we must seek throughout the world for the treasures of which the second is composed. They are the blessings which God's goodness has bestowed on man. Like aromatic gums, having been sought with loving diligence, they must be pounded in the mortar of the heart with the pestle of meditation, brought to a great heat by the fire of holy desire, and mixed with the oil of gladness. Such a perfume will infinitely excel the former. This it is of which God says in the Psalm: "The sacrifice of praise shall honour Me;" for of the other it is only said that God will not despise it. This must be far better which He says shall honour Him. The first is poured upon the feet, the second upon the head. Now the head of Christ is God, and to give thanks is to perfume the Head, for, although God and man are one Christ, all blessing comes from God, even that which comes through man. For this, the Scripture condemns whoso puts his trust in man; for, though all our hope be in Christ, it is not because He is man, but because He is God.

The penitent who knows that his former sins are still alive within him, who can only think of rooting out these thorns, who is weary with sighs and tears, he cannot take his flight and rise to the contemplation of God's gifts and blessings. He has read that praise is hateful in the mouth of a sinner, he knows that in his heart, full of sorrow, it would be discordant, like "music in mourning." Moreover, thanksgiving follows, not precedes a gift, and such a heart is gasping for a favour, the gift of forgiveness; it sees only darkness, and no light; it feels only bitterness; and the sad remembrance of sins excludes all thoughts of joy.

This second perfume is clearly not for such hearts. We may learn from the example of the Apostles who they are that may offer it in abundance. "They went out from the Council rejoicing that they were accounted worthy to suffer reproach for the name of Jesus;" their sweetness had been unmoved either by words or blows, they had ample store of this spiritual unction. Their hearts indeed gave forth a delicious odour when, "going forth, they published the glory of God in various tongues as the Spirit gave them utterance." But for us all this perfume is most desirable because it alleviates the weariness of life; the celebration of God's praises brings an imitation on earth of the joys of the blessed. I therefore counsel you, you that I love, frequently to lay aside the bitter saddening consideration of your sins, and to fill your hearts with happy thoughts of God's goodness. We are bound indeed to have grief, but not continually; and it ought to be mingled with the grateful remembrance of God's clemency, lest too great sadness should stiffen the heart, and despair take hold of it to its ruin. If Cain had so recollected God's goodness, he would not have said: "My iniquity is greater than that I may deserve pardon." God forbid we should ever so imagine, for His goodness is greater far than any crime. The more lowly your thoughts are of yourselves, the more trustful may be your reliance on God's sovereign goodness. If we shut out from our hearts thoughts of gratitude and praise, how shall we obey the Apostle: "In all things give thanks"? We shall rather come under the shameful condemnation: "They forgot His benefits and the wonders that He had shown them." At the least let us never forget the very greatest of all His works, our redemption—let that never be absent from our minds. There are two chief points in it for our recollection. First, how (to use the Apostle's words) "God emptied Himself;" and then, how we are thereby filled with Him. To think on that awakens us to holy hope. To dwell on this kindles our hearts to ardent love. Both are indispensable; lest our hope, not being mingled with love, be mercenary, or our love cold, unmixed with hope. What do we hope for from our love? It is that which He who is the object of our love has promised in these words: "Good measure, pressed down, heaped up and running over, shall be given to you." But what shall be thus measured? "Eye hath not seen, O God, besides Thee, what things Thou hast prepared for them that wait for Thee." What things? Corn, wine, and oil, gold, silver, precious stones? These all we have seen; we see them now, and scorn them. We seek what it "hath not entered into the heart of man to conceive." Behold that is our hope; that, whatever it be, is our desire. That is none else than God Himself, who shall be our "all in all." The fulness we desire is God, and all God. Who can tell the ineffable sweetness that lies in these words: "God shall be all in all"!

In the soul there are three powers—reason, memory, and will. Every thinking person knows that he is wanting and imperfect. Why, but because God is not yet all in all; because the reason is often deceived, the will torn and troubled by passion, the memory confused? How mournful for a being so noble to be subject to this triple weakness, although it have a hope of deliverance. He that shall fulfil the desires of the soul with every good shall be Himself, to the reason, Light never failing; Peace beyond understanding to the will; to the memory, its eternal, ever-present Object. O Truth, O Love, O Eternity! O Trinity most blessed and source of benediction! The miserable trinity within me sighs because, to her exceeding loss, she is separated from thee! And yet, why this sadness and dejection? "Put thy trust in God, for I will yet give Him thanks." Error shall be cleared from my intelligence, suffering from my will, and fear from my memory, when the marvellous serenity, the perfect sweetness, and the eternal safety that we hope for, shall have taken their place. The Truth, which is God, shall do the first; the Love, which is God, the second; and the Almighty Power, which is God, the third; so shall God be all in all. The reason shall be flooded with inextinguishable light; the will shall enjoy a peace no turmoil can ever ruffle; the memory shall draw for ever from an inexhaustible spring of happiness.

Let us now consider the mode of our redemption, and in the effacement of the divinity of God chiefly three points. It was no small thing. He was made flesh. He died. It was upon the Cross. How can we realise in any measure the excess of humility, of sweetness, of ineffable goodness, which caused the Sovereign Majesty to take flesh, to suffer death, to die dishonoured on the tree? It may be asked: Was not the Creator able to repair His work without such humbling of Himself? He was able; but He loved best to do it by suffering, that man might never more have an excuse for ingratitude. He endured such torments for us that we might owe Him endless love, and that the labour of our redemption might constrain those to gratitude whom creation (done with but a word) had failed to touch. For though we owe God unbounded gratitude for the free gift of existence, that indeed cost Him nothing. But, O miserable man, who can question the price He paid for our redemption? He disdained not to be as a slave, though Himself supreme Master; to be poor, though possessed of all; to be flesh, though Himself the Word of God; to be the Son of man, although He was the Son of God. In six days He made all creation; but He gave thirty years to the work of our salvation. He bore the infirmity of the flesh, and the temptations of the enemy. He perfected all by the horror of death, and the ignominy of the Cross.

Ponder these things in your mind. Cease not to think of them. Pour out such perfumes in your heart that they may overcome the vile stench of your sins which has so long been an offence to Him.

But there remains another perfume far surpassing either of these two. I call it piety. It is made up of the wants of the poor, the woes of the oppressed, the affliction of the sorrowful, and all the troubles of the unhappy, be they who they may, even our enemies. These seem but humble ingredients; yet their union is most sweet to the heavenly Bridegroom. Happy the soul which can offer the ointment they compose. "Acceptable is the man who showeth mercy and lendeth;" he who is moved by the wants of others and eager to relieve them; whose delight is to bestow; who forgives readily, and is not easily provoked; who never revenges a wrong, and feels the woes of others as if they were his own. Happy one, the dew of mercy lies upon your soul; you are filled full of charity; you make yourself all to all, that you may help all in every time and place; you are dead to self and live for others. That is indeed the rarest and most acceptable offering which shall distil from your hands and delight your God. No smallest sacrifice will He forget, but will receive your holocaust and perfect it.

Was not St. Paul rich in this costly perfume; who was everywhere the sweet savour of Christ; who generously cared for all the churches; who died daily for the glory of God; who, as a mother, fed the babes of Christ with the sincere milk of the Word; who "travailed in birth-pangs" again and again until the Saviour was formed in them, until some likeness could be seen in them to their Head? Or look at Job, who could say of himself, "I was an eye to the blind, and a foot to the lame; I was a father to the poor; they waited for me as for rain." Each one of his actions was a perfume. Joseph, again, who, after having fed all Egypt, would also give to the brethren who had sold him; and, though he looked at them with a severe countenance, his tears showed the love which filled his heart. Samuel wept for Saul, who desired to kill him, out of the piety that overflowed his heart, so that all Israel knew him for the faithful prophet of the Lord. And what of Moses, of whom the Holy Spirit has borne witness that he was "exceeding meek above all the men that dwelt in the earth"? "With men that hated peace he was peaceable," and interceded for them, when God was angry, so vehemently as to say: "Forgive them this trespass; or, if Thou do not, strike me out of the book which Thou hast written." He would not enter into the joy of the Lord, leaving the people without, whom, though they were ungrateful, he cherished with the tenderness of a mother.

The perfumes of these holy souls smell sweetly to this day in the Church. It shall be so with all who in this life have been merciful and loving, have not sought their own, but have made all free to all they had; esteeming this their duty, as well to enemies as friends, to the foolish as to the wise; humble beyond all, helpful to all, beloved above all, both of God and men. All such sent forth an odour of sweetness in their own day which still perfumes the world in ours. Of such an one it shall be said: "This is a lover of his brethren, and of the people of Israel; this is he that prayeth much for the people, and for the holy city." Furthermore, we read in the Gospel of the holy woman who bought sweet spices to embalm the body of the Lord; not to anoint the feet, nor yet the head alone, but the whole body—to embalm Jesus. In like manner I would have you all, not merely fulfil the duties of charity to your kindred and your friends, to those that have done good to you, or from whom you have any hope of benefit (for the heathen do as much as this), but to all, even to your enemies. Be sure that this will make you to abound in exquisite perfumes, and to anoint, so far as in you lies, Christ's whole Sacred Body, which is the Church. The Lord Jesus waited not in the grave for the spices prepared for His dead body. Was it to save them for His living one, for the Church? This is the body dearest to Him it is plain; for we know that He gave up the other to death, but the Church He keeps alive by the Bread which came down from heaven.

To speak for a moment of myself. It has happened to me at times to be reproached. Either I have been sitting at the feet of Jesus, for my own soul's good, weeping over the bitter remembrance of my sins; or, a rarer case with me, I have been standing at His Head, rejoicing in His praise; and I have heard it said: Wherefore is this waste? I have been accused of living for myself alone, and upbraided because it was thought that I ought to be doing more for others. Now the truth is this: How would it profit me to gain the world, if I lose my own soul? I have remembered the words of God in Scripture: "My people, they who call thee happy deceive thee;" and I liken such speakers to the flies that corrupt the ointment and perish in it. Let those who find fault with my quietness hear the Lord answer for me: "Why torment ye this woman?" That is: You can only see the outside arid judge thereby; this is not such a man as you imagine, but rather a woman; why lay upon him a yoke he is not able to bear? He is doing a good work to Me. He is doing what he can, not being able for more. When he has come to man's perfect strength, he will do a man's full work. For like reason none should ever criticise or reproach a bishop. Great is his dignity, very great his burden. It is inhuman to censure the conduct of those whose work we could not do. How could a woman knitting at home criticise the actions of a soldier on service? Remember that to go forth to fight is itself a manly, admirable thing. If a soldier has his imperfections, remember that charity covers a multitude of sins; his self-devotion stands him in good stead and pleads for him.

But to return from this digression to the perfumes of the Bride. You perceive how that of piety is the most beloved of all; so loved that not one particle of it shall perish; even a cup of cold water shall not be without its reward. By this most blessed piety is the body of the Lord anointed, and I say not that body which He gave up to be crucified, but that which, by His sufferings, He redeemed.

But who is he that shall claim to contain these precious things in his soul? Who even will dare to say that he has so much as the first one in perfection? But the Church possesses all. Who dares to claim fully for his own soul the name of Bride of Christ? Not any one would so presume. But the Church is the Bride of our Lord, and we who are her members, and glory in so being, we surely have some right to participate in her high calling and her name. Thanks be to Thee, O Saviour, Jesus Christ, who hast deigned to make us members of that body so beloved, I mean not only Christians, but, in virtue of that union, Brides of God, with the hope of nuptials spiritual and eternal hereafter, when with open face we shall behold Thee in Thy glory, wherein Thou art co-equal with the Father and the Holy Ghost for ever.

The heavenly Spouse is called by many names in Holy Scripture; but all are in one or other of two classes. Either they express the riches of His goodness, or the greatness of His majesty. The Holy Spirit declares by David: "Two things have I heard; that power belongeth unto God, and mercy unto Thee, O Lord." Some relate to His supreme powers, some to His sovereign mercy, of which may it not be said it is "as oil poured forth"? It is in those of our Saviour Jesus Christ. If we study we shall see that in every one the name of majesty is made to melt into a name of tenderness. The name of God, does it not sweetly pass into "Emmanuel, God with us," and the like? The voice of thunder and the word "I am the Lord thy God" has been softened into Father, the first of all words for us Christians. Of slaves we are made friends; and the news of the resurrection is sent, not only to the disciples, but to "My brethren." It is by the sufferings of Jesus and His resurrection that this has come to pass, and by the preaching in His name of repentance and the remission of sins that, at the name of Christ, the multitude of the faithful should become Christians. This is the name of which Isaiah said: "The Lord God shall call His servants by another name in which he that is blest upon the earth shall be blessed in God. Amen." As oil it has flowed from heaven to earth and over all the earth, and even into hell; for it is written again that "In the name of Jesus every knee shall bow, of those that are in heaven, on earth, and under the earth;" and that every tongue should confess that "Thy name is as oil poured forth." I have my part in this name, for I am a Christian and the brother of Jesus Christ. I am "heir of God, and joint-heir with Christ." Not only His name is poured forth, but Himself; for He saith: "I am poured out like water." The fulness of the divinity was poured forth on earth when the word of God took a mortal body, that we in our bodies of death might partake of His fulness and cry out: "Thy name is as oil poured forth." His pouring forth is as oil, because oil enlightens, nourishes, and heals. From whence was that great, sudden light that illuminated the world, but from the preaching of the name of Jesus? It is in "Thy light that we see light." Oil also is food and nourishment. Herein is it like the name of Jesus! How dry and worthless is everything without it. A book has no interest for me if I find not there the word Jesus. Conversation has no charm if Jesus form no part of it. That name is as honey to the mouth, as melody to the ears, a song of gladness to the heart.

It is also a remedy. Is any sad? Let the name of Jesus come into his mind and pass upon his lips. No sooner is that name of power pronounced than a light appears, so glorious that it drives away all clouds, and gives back tranquil peace. Does the remorse of a crime pursue a soul? Is such an one ready to rush to death for deliverance from torment? Let him call upon the name of Jesus, and the breath of life returns to him. With this adorable name in his heart, who ever persisted in revenge, sloth, languor, hardness? Who has not felt the rush of salutary tears bless him once more when he has cried to Jesus? Who ever has invoked that strong and generous name, when his heart was beating in the midst of fear and danger, and not felt quietness come down upon him? Who, when wavering in miserable perplexity and doubt, has called upon the name of Jesus without receiving calming light into his soul? Who, borne down and discouraged by long adversity, has not found new courage come to him by use of that all-helpful name? These are the infirmities of the soul, and this their fitting remedy. It is written: "Call upon Me in the time of trouble. I will deliver you and you shall honour Me." No other thing can, like that holy name, quell the madness of anger, bring down the swelling of pride, heal the sores of envy, allay the torment of impurity, destroy the lust of greed, appease the thirst of avarice, and arrest unruly or shameful thoughts; for when I name the name of Jesus it is not only that I recall the image of a man meek and humble of heart, kind, gentle, chaste, and merciful, full of all sorts of goodness, but I remember Him as God the Almighty. All this is in the name of Jesus; and whoso will not love it deserves death and is dead. Whoso lives not for Jesus lives for nought, and is nothing; for man is merest nothingness unless he know God. God has proved His love for us to be tender, wise, and strong; tender, for He truly became man; wise, for He only made as if He were a sinner; strong, in that He has confounded the wiles of the evil one. And after the same manner we must love our Lord; tenderly, that sinful love may be thereby expelled; wisely, for His love must be not only in our hearts but in our minds, lest we be seduced by the spirit of deceit, or our lives be indiscreet and immoderate; and mighty, that our lives may be steadfast and generous, fearless and persevering.

There is a merely human love for God: the love of the heart for the humanity of Jesus Christ. We may believe it was to attract this love that God, who is invisible, became man, and, as man, dwelt on earth, to enable carnal men to love Him carnally, and so to draw them on. To love our Lord Jesus Christ with all the heart, is to love His sacred Body, His humanity, better than our own, than all the world, than anything we love in it. But, though such affection be a gift and a great gift of the Holy Ghost, there is a higher love than this by far; for Jesus Christ has been made to us wisdom, justice, sanctification, and redemption, and to love Him as such is better than to love the earthly life of Jesus, and to weep with sympathy over His sufferings, though this be well; for thereby the life of the flesh is overcome and the world despised and vanquished. The human love for Jesus is as the overshadowing of Mary when the glory of the Holy Ghost came down upon her. It is impossible to love the manhood of our Lord without the Holy Ghost; yet it is rather for those who are still imperfect, as the Apostle says: "We have known Christ according to the flesh, but now we know Him so no longer;" for that is a carnal affection compared with the love of the Word, Wisdom; the Word, Justice; the Word, Truth; the Word, Holiness, Piety, Virtue, and all His other perfections. No speciousness of the devil or of heresy can make such love falter from the smallest teaching of the Church. This is the love of God with all the soul. And if to this be joined such strength, such power from the Holy Ghost, that neither torments, nor the fear of death, nor death itself, can make us fail in justice, then we love God with all our strength, and this is spiritual love, the entire being loving without measure, filled with the Holy Ghost.

When the Church, the Bride, beheld her Beloved ascend up into heaven, did she not passionately long to go with Him and be received into His glory? It is the cry of every holy soul clogged with the imperfections of this evil time, and hindered from her joy: "Draw me;" for "the corruptible body is a load upon the soul, and the earthly habitation presseth down the mind." "Unhappy man that I am, who shall deliver me from the body of this death?" "Bring my soul out of prison." But not only so; the Bride asks still more than this: the grace to imitate her Spouse, to follow in His steps, to love by the same rule as He, to be made perfect like Him. She longs to forget herself, and to bear her cross, and she knows His words: "Without Me ye can do nothing." Many, nay all, desire to die the death of the just, and enjoy after this life the eternal joys that are with Jesus. All desire this end, but many abhor the way to it. Only the loving and beloved desire to follow Him whithersoever He goeth. The Bride is strong, and brave, and beautiful, ready for all. She shrinks from nothing. She would say: "O Beloved, what Thou wilt—temptation, suffering, chastisement, what Thou wilt, till I may see Thy face. It is in thine own strength that Thou goest, O Lord, the strength as of a mighty man of war, for God, Thy God, hath anointed Thee with the oil of gladness above Thy fellows; but we never run but in the odour of Thy perfumes; the strength and the running is all from Thee." There are seasons when the soul runs easily, and an eager zeal to be with Christ makes sacrifice delightful and all exertion sweet. In such times let no one say: "I shall never be moved;" lest he soon have to lament, "Thou turnedst Thy face from me and I became troubled." And when weariness shall have fallen upon the spirit, and in darkness and dreariness life is a burden, be not cast down; feel for His hand who can lift you up, call upon Him like the Bride, say to Him: "Draw me, we will run;" so shall hope support you in the days of heaviness, and foresight prepare you against trouble, and your soul shall be like eternity; as in the days of old it shall be the image of God in whom there is no change, neither shadow of turning; through Him you shall recover man's ancient glory, and you shall neither grovel in adversity nor shall prosperity elate you, but all shall work together for your good. Need we wonder that the Bride cries, "Draw me," when He whom she has to follow is as a giant rejoicing to run His course, leaping over the mountains? But, drawn by Him, she will run; and, not only so; the soul that is so beautiful and happy as to know His love, will not only run herself, but will draw others after her; we will run. For charity desires always that others should share her gifts; and they who are with the Bride, see her example and hear her words, are fired with like desire and run with her.

God only knows the delights the Holy Ghost reveals to His beloved, by what inspiration He awakens and recruits the senses of the soul, and with what odours He refreshes it. This is "a garden closed, a fountain sealed," but the waste water runs through public places, and at these I may quench my thirst, and then give drink to others. The water runs in four great streams; or, to return to the former figure, the Church is refreshed by four rare perfumes whose ingredients are all heavenly, and they fill the whole house, attracting the beloved from the four quarters of the world, as the Queen of Sheba came from afar to hear the wisdom of Solomon, drawn by the odour of his reputation. Let us search into the mystery of these four perfumes, and try to know somewhat of the abundant ineffable fragrance of Him whom the Father hath anointed with the oil of gladness.

The world sat in darkness and the shadow of death when He arrived to deliver it. He dispersed the shades of night by the illumination of His wisdom. By the justice which comes of faith He broke the chains of the captives, giving them free pardon. Among a sinful people He lived holily, and thus marked out a way for their return to the lost home. He gave Himself up to death, appeased the Father by the satisfaction He offered, and by the five wounds of the cross poured forth the abundant redemption He had won for us. By wisdom, justice, sanctification, and redemption, He has filled the whole world with His fragrance, and having gone up on high, He has by them drawn all men after Him. By these four—Remember them. By constant meditation draw out their deep, mysterious sweetness, as God may please to reveal it to you, for to analyse these perfumes is beyond the power of man. The fulness of Jesus Christ is past all finding out. The wisdom of God is infinite, His justice like the great mountains, His sanctification incomparable, and His redemption perfect.

We have seen that they are the souls urged by love that run. The Bride runs, her companions also; but she, for that she loves much, runs fastest, reaches first, and is first admitted—but her charity, her solicitude and tender anxiety forbid her ever to forget her children in the Gospel; she encourages them, tells them of her happiness, and they too run and enter, after her, the "store-rooms of the King." What may be the meaning of these words? We read of His garden, His store-rooms, His chamber. By the help of the Holy Spirit let us explain the difference between them. Let the garden stand for the simple words of Holy Scripture; the store-rooms, their moral sense; and the chamber, the secrets of God which are attained by sublime contemplation.

I do not claim to have experience of these, or to glory in a prerogative reserved for the Bride alone; but each soul of the beloved of the King has its own secret with Him; some little I have learnt; and for the rest, may God, with whom is all knowledge, teach it you. The penitent woman had her place at the feet of our Lord; another, if it be another, at His head. St. Thomas was admitted to the wound of the side of Jesus; St. John to lie upon His breast; St. Peter to the bosom of the Father; St. Paul to the third heaven. Who shall say where lies the cause of these diversities? It may be the first penitent was there through her humility; the second, through the vehemence of hope; St. Thomas in the strength of faith; St. John by the trustfulness of his love; St. Paul in the depth of his wisdom; St. Peter in the illumination of truth. There are many mansions; and each is placed according to his secret, to abide till he shall enter further into the joy of his Lord, into the ineffable mysteries of the Spouse. How little have I ever entered into that rest, and for how little time have I stayed! In that chamber is the sense of God's eternal mercies towards those that fear Him. Happy indeed, and truly happy he whose sins God will not lay to his charge. To be justified it needs but to have His favour whom we have offended. Not to sin belongs to God alone. The indulgence of God is man's justice. It is written: "Whosoever is born of God committeth not sin, because He is born of God;" that is, in the eternal predestination and favour of God, their sins are as not existing. In time, they may have been, in eternity they do not appear; the infinite charity of God covering their multitude. O blessed chamber of God's perfect love! If ever it should be your happy lot, any one of you, to be admitted for a little season into this divine mysterious sanctuary, give praise and say: "The King hath brought me into His chamber." I do not say it need be the most secret, intimate, of all. Still it is a chamber, the chamber of the King; less wonderful than restful, sweet, serene and tranquil.

But though the saints thus contemplate with open face God's glory, and are changed into His image as St. Paul was rapt into the third heaven, having in his admirable purity passed through the first and second, their outward seeming still remains, like his, vile and abject. This I think is meant when the Bride says: "I am black, but comely;" black in the judgment of man, comely in the sight of God and holy angels. Within the soul of the saints is the brightness of eternal light, and they care not to delight man; knowing that they please God whose favour only they desire. They even "glory in their infirmities," and in being reproached, like Him of whom it was said that He had "no beauty in Him nor comeliness," yet was He beautiful above the sons of men. So the Church is reviled and despised, and not without just cause; for in her exile she cannot fail to be stained with many spots, and wrinkled, wounded and wearied, tanned and discoloured, black externally like the tents of Cedar, which word means darkness; but, within, "The king's daughter is all glorious," like the "tabernacle the true Solomon hath set in the sun," like the "heaven He hath stretched out as a pavilion." The heavens are not too high to be compared to her, for is not her spiritual being heavenly? And what more heavenly proof of a celestial origin can there be than, in an animal, ignoble body, to live the life of angels, adoring God and loving Jesus Christ supremely? Is a soul that can do this of earth? The heavens which are like her beauty are not resplendent only with gorgeous tints, but glorious with all beatitudes. Some of the blessed shall be "as the brightness of the firmament," and others shall shine as the stars for all eternity;" and each such soul in which God has set up His tabernacle is a heaven, to which the material heavens cannot be compared, for its perfection is all spiritual, and what thing is there that can equal the excellence of a soul which has put on its heavenly beauty, is decked with virtues like costly pearls, is more ethereal than the air, more splendid than the dazzling sun? The beauty of such a soul is charity, justice, patience, poverty, faith, humility and the like, whose reward is an eternal kingdom and a glory that shall have no end.

This which I have said of the Saints is true also of our Lord. "His look was hidden and despised, and we esteemed him not;" but within was the glory of His divinity and the brightness of His innocence. Did not some hidden splendour pierce through the veil of misery and apparent sin when the centurion cried out: "Indeed this man was the Son of God"? The soldier heard him "cry with a loud voice;" and, though he saw Him die upon the cross, he declared this man was the Son of God; for faith comes by hearing. The centurion heeded not the lying testimony of the eyes. He heard and believed, and confessed. By the hearing, sin first entered into man, and now by the hearing of faith life is restored. By faith is the truth received and confessed. By faith is the eye purified, and the reward of faith is the Beatific Vision. The natural eye sees but the blackness of the "curtains of Solomon," the disgrace of the flesh which He assumed for us; faith apprehends His divine, surpassing beauty, which even when allowed to transpierce His mortal body, so transfigured it that the eyes of the Apostles could not bear the glory. Faith discerns God in the flesh, life in death, the fulness of adorable majesty in the midst of shame, the purity of innocence and the splendour of holiness within the cloud of apparent sin. By this revelation of faith the Bride, the Church, is humbled to bitter repentance for the sins which have spoilt her fairness; compared to her Beloved, she feels herself dark indeed. She yearns for Him and to be like Him, and her tears and the weariness of penance take all her brightness from her. She thinks she has done nothing for Him. "My own vine have I not kept". She gazes upon His perfections, till all in herself seems neglect and fault. She gazes upon Him, and the more fixed her gaze, the more she desires the presence of "Him whom her soul loveth." "Show me where Thou feedest, where Thou liest in the mid-day." I would fain explain to you how the words of the Bride are good for every one of us, according to the state and aspirations of our heart; but this is extremely difficult, for we possess no expressions but those which concern material things, and in those which are only and wholly spiritual how unworthy they are and open to misconstruction!

"No man hath seen God at any time." To neither Saint nor Prophet has it ever been possible in this mortal body to see God as He is. Only hereafter, when we shall have put on immortality and our nature is become spiritual, shall we be able to see God; for He is the "I Am," the sole existence; to whom there is neither past nor future, but eternity, the perpetual present. Still there are many ways in which God is pleased to manifest Himself in this mortal life, as by the beautiful and marvellous works of creation, and, as to the patriarchs, under various forms. Above all, God has another way by which He reveals Himself, more rare by far, because wholly interior and spiritual. This vision is never given but to souls that seek God and desire His coming, with burning desire that burns up all impurity of sin: "a fire shall go before Him and shall burn up His enemies round about;" thus is a place prepared for the Lord. There are seasons at which God vouchsafes to visit such souls, and they know that the Lord is near when they feel such a kindling within them, for, "from above He hath sent fire into my bones." This is the visit of God and His union with the soul meant by the Apostle when he says: "He that is joined to the Lord is one spirit." We express as best we can how a pure soul is ravished in God, the blessed descent of God into it. God is spirit, and it is in spirit that He comes, for He is spiritual love for the spiritual beauty of that blessed soul which He sees to be walking in the way of holiness and to be loving Him wholly and alone. The supreme desire of a soul so beloved by God is that God should come to her, not to her bodily sight, as He has sometimes deigned to appear to His servants under one form or another, but that He should penetrate and fill her; for the word of God speaks not to the ears, but pierces the heart; He is not eloquent, but efficacious. There is no similitude which may be seen, but He transfigures the soul and fills the heart with the joy which springs from love. Yet even so I do not say that a soul can see Him as He is. Each soul differs from each, and the savour of the divine presence differs also in each recipient. To some He is a friend walking with them by the way, making their hearts burn within them by His talk; to some as their Father, in a home of plenty, providing every need; to some as a Bridegroom, caressing and embracing His Bride; to some as a Physician restoring with oil and wine, refreshing with aromatic perfumes; to some as a sovereign Prince comforting his wife who is poor and timid, showing her all his precious things, admitting her even to His secret cabinet, caring not to hide anything from her whose lowlihead He has not despised, whose fidelity He has proved, whose beauty is to Him so dear that he covers her with kisses.

Under every seeming He is full of charm, of sweetness and of mercy; clement, gay, affable and gracious; liberal and royal. In these among many ways our

Lord reveals Himself to hearts that seek Him, as He promised: "I am with you all days, even to the consummation of the world." And yet it is not now as it shall be hereafter. This life is but the shadow of the life to come; "we see as in a glass darkly, but then face to face; we know in part and we divine in part;" "under Thy shadow we live," for faith is the shadow of good things to come. The just live by faith, and the blessed see God. It is good to apprehend these great things; let us therefore try with prayer and the assistance of the Holy Spirit to enter into that which, as He deigns to do it for mortals by His indwelling, He may give us to understand by His illumination.

If then some soul should come to know that it is well to be closely united to God, or (to speak more clearly) if any should feel like the Apostle a desire to be rid of this mortal flesh and to be with Jesus, with a living, vehement desire, a burning thirst in his heart for God, the living God, we believe that our Lord will surely come to such an one as a Bridegroom, will take such a soul into His arms and shed abroad in her heart the sweetness of divine love; the heart's longing shall be satisfied, its thirst shall be quenched, even though it possess its joy but for a moment and imperfectly; for if He be sought with sighs, tears, prayers and watchings, and at last do come to the soul, suddenly, while He seems to be present, He is gone; yet again if His loss be lamented with desolate seeking up and down, if the devout soul persevere in prayer, He will not let her ask in vain, He will suffer Himself once more to be found, yet not to be detained. His coming is for a moment, and, though it entrance the soul with delight, His departure brings back sadness; and so in alternate joy and sorrow shall the Bride ever be, until that all-glorious time when, having laid down this heavy, terrestrial body, she goes (flying as it were on the wings of desire) to the perpetual freedom of the contemplation of the Beloved, following Him in spirit whithersoever He goeth, free from all let and hindrance.

But remember that only to few souls, those that have great devotion, vehement aspiration, and a love for God as trustful as it is tender, to only such does the Lord vouchsafe to appear as to a living and beloved Bride. He has other manifestations for other characters. To one who, pierced with compunction by the thought of his sins, prays to God in the bitterness of his soul not to condemn him, or to one still battling with fierce temptations, the Lord will appear as a Physician full of healing. Can we not bear witness to this from our own experience? Have we never wept, thinking it was beyond hope that such as we could be saved? and, of a sudden, the hope of pardon, the joy of forgiveness, have slid into our soul. Yet, if we should not remember, let us trust to His testimony, for He says: "The Spirit of the Lord is upon me, the Lord hath anointed me to heal the contrite of heart, and to preach a release to the captives." Again there are others who, weary of their spiritual exercises, fall into laxity and indifference, walking wearily in the way of the Lord with a dry, dull heart, feeling that the days and nights are long. If the Lord, moved with compassion, draws near to such an one, and He who is from heaven begins to tell of heavenly things, to sing some delicious song of Sion, to speak of the city of peace, the eternity of its delights, the happiness of attaining to them, such inspirations soothe and rouse the soul, dispel all lassitude and sloth, and awaken both body and spirit to begin afresh. When you are conscious of such things within you, think not that the change is from yourself; remember who it is that saith: "It is I that speak justice and am a defender to save." For He also teacheth us in the Gospel: "From the heart come forth evil thoughts;" and again by the Apostle: "We are not sufficient to think anything as of ourselves; but our sufficiency is of God;" and the Psalmist saith: "I will hear what the Lord God shall say in my heart."

All good thought is the visit of the Word of God: "without me ye can do nothing." Be therefore careful that His grace in you be not void. There are again hearts to whom the Lord appears as a Father or as a Sovereign; hearts I think magnanimous and brave, which have acquired through special purity of conscience a free, courageous, enterprising spirit. These are capable of bold undertakings, and are not satisfied until, by a praiseworthy curiosity, they have penetrated and understood the most secret and sublime things, and attained to the most perfect virtue. For the greatness of their faith makes them worthy of the plenitude of all good, and there is nothing in the treasure of wisdom from which the God of wisdom holds it fitting to exclude them. These are heroic souls, on fire with love of truth, and exempt from all vanity. Such was Moses, who dared to say to God: "If I have found favour in thy sight, show me thy face;" and such David, who said: "Thy face will I seek." Such souls dare to aspire to great things because they themselves are great. To such, God says that He will give all the ground that they tread upon; for their great faith merits great reward, and they take possession of whatever realms they cover with the feet of hope. The heavenly Spouse shows Himself indeed to these souls: He entertains them magnificently with His light and His truth, and so leads them into His holy mountain and His tabernacle, that they may truly say, with the Blessed Virgin: "He that is mighty has done great things to me."

* * * * *

* * * * *

"Show me, O Thou whom my soul loveth, where thou feedest Thy flock, where Thou reposest in the noonday." How shall I attain to see thee and myself with thee; thou feeding in the mountains those ninety-nine sheep which the shepherd leaves there when he goes to seek the one which has wandered? It is with good reason that the Spouse sighs and aspires after the place which is at once a pasture and a place of rest and security, of joy, wonder, and astonishment. Hapless am I that I can only salute it from afar. On the shores of the rivers of Babylon we weep, remembering thee, O Sion. Who but must fervently desire to feed in this pasture, that he may taste peace, and feed to satiety on the fine flour of wheat? This secure abode is Paradise, this delicious nourishment is our Lord Himself, and this great abundance is eternity. Let us hasten, then, my children, towards that sure dwelling, those delightful fields. For here, Lord, Thou pasturest, indeed, Thy sheep, but Thou dost not satisfy them. It is not here permitted to rest; we must stand upright, and watch because of the terrors of the night. Alas, this light is not pure, this food is not sufficient nor all-sweet, this abode is not safe. Show me, then, where Thou pasturest Thy flock, reposing in the noontide. Thou callest me blessed, because I hunger and thirst after justice; but what is that compared with the felicity of those upon whom are heaped the treasures of Thy house, who are always seated at Thy banquet, and rejoice for ever in Thy presence? If I suffer anything for justice' sake, Thou sayest again that I am happy; but to pasture and to suffer at the same time, is not that a poor felicity? I possess here everything except perfection; many things happen beyond my hopes, but nothing is sure. Teach me where Thou reposest at noontide. I know well enough where Thou pasturest without reposing.

There are, O Lord, other shepherds besides Thee who call themselves Thy companions, and are not so; who have flocks of their own, and meadows full of poisonous herbs, in which they feed their charge, but without Thee and without Thy orders. These are they who say: "Christ is here," and "Christ is there." They promise fertile fields of wisdom and knowledge; men believe them, and run in crowds to them; but these shepherds make those who follow them to be children of the devil even more than they themselves are. And why? Because here is no noonday, nor pure light, in which the truth can be known clearly. Here falsehood is often mistaken for truth, because in the obscurity the difference is not easily detected. For my part, I think that we should sigh after the noontide, not only for these causes, but also, and above all, on account of the artifices of invisible powers, of seducing spirits who ever lie in ambush with their arrows made ready to pierce those who are of an upright heart. For, in this obscurity, Satan transforms himself into an angel of light, and we can only be safe from the noonday fiend by dwelling in the noonday. Great is the temptation when the evil to which we are tempted is made to appear a great good. This is the temptation of the perfect, of those brave and generous souls who have surmounted all—pleasures, vainglory, and honours. It would be useless to tempt such persons openly; so the demon comes concealed under the semblance of some good. The more perfect the soul, the greater her need of caution against such danger. Hence the Blessed Virgin was troubled at the salutation of the angel. She fancied at first that it might be some deceit of the enemy. Hence, also, Joshua would not receive the angel as friendly to him until he had interrogated him; and our Lord's disciples feared to see Him walking to them on the sea, until He cried: "It is I, do not fear." In reward of our caution, the true Noonday thus speaks, lest, in such temptations, we take darkness for light or light for darkness.

"If thou know not thyself, O fairest among women, go forth, and follow after the steps of the flocks, and feed thy kids beside the tents of the shepherds." Moses, presuming too much on the grace and familiarity of God, asked for a great vision. But, instead of this, a lesser was given him, by which, nevertheless, he should by and by be able to attain his desire. The sons of Zebedee were in like manner rebuked. And so the Spouse, having asked a great thing, finds herself reproved and humbled by a reply full of severity and love. For, in proportion as one aspires to great things, one must think little of one's self. Extraordinary graces are given only to extraordinary humility; and he who is destined to receive them will always be prepared by sharp abasement. When, therefore, you are greatly humbled, take it for a sign that the grace of God is nigh at hand. But, remember that it is humility, not humiliation, which profits. How many are humiliated without becoming humble! Some are soured by humiliations, some bear them patiently, others receive them with joy. The first are guilty, the second innocent, but the third sort alone are just, and receive the reward of humiliation.

There is no attaining to God without self-knowledge; for from such knowledge alone come humility and the fear of God, which is the beginning of salvation as well as of wisdom. But you must also know God; for how shall we love Him if we do not know Him, possess Him if we do not love Him? To know yourself is to fear God; to know Him is to love Him. The one is the beginning of wisdom, the other of perfection. Ignorance on these points is fatal. All other knowledge is indifferent. We are not saved by having it, nor lost for want of it.

If any one could know clearly himself as God knows him, the duty of each would be to esteem himself neither too lowly nor too highly, but in this, as in all things, to acquiesce in the truth. But since it has pleased God to conceal from us our own condition, insomuch that it is written that no one can tell whether he is worthy of love or of hate, it is wiser and safer always to choose the lowest place; for it is better to be called up higher than to be obliged to take with shame an inferior seat. There is no harm in thinking too little, even much too little, of yourself; but there is a horrible danger in raising yourself in the least degree above that which you in truth are. In passing through a low door, however lowly you carry your head, you have nothing to fear; but, bear it only an inch too high, and you will be painfully informed of your own stature.

So much for ignorance of ourselves. What now is the consequence of the ignorance of God? To know ourselves and not to know God, is to despair. A man returning to himself, and feeling a disgust for all the ill he has committed, thinks to depart from his evil way and from all the disorders of a life according to the senses. But, if he does not know how good God is, how kind and favourable and willing to pardon, his carnal thoughts will check him, saying: What are you doing? Do you want to lose this life as well as the next? Your sins are too great and numerous. If you were to tear your body to pieces, it would not be sufficient expiation. Your nature is delicate, you have always lived softly; how can you expect to oppose with success the customs of your life? Cast into despondency by these and the like thoughts, he returns to his disorders, not knowing with how great ease the Almighty can remove all such obstacles. Thus the ignorance of God produces that consummation of all wickedness, despair.

All who will not be converted must be ignorant of God. For, if they refuse, it can only be because they fancy Him severe and rigorous when He is kind, inexorable whereas He is full of pity, cruel and terrible while He is all-amiable. Souls of little faith, what do you fear? You fancy that, being angered by the enormity and multitude of your crimes, He would delay to stretch out to you His helping hand. But know that grace commonly superabounds where sin has abounded, God's love being, in consideration of their necessities, more obviously manifested to penitents who have sinned greatly than to those who have sinned less.

God forbid, however, that we should think it is this kind of ignorance against which He warns His Spouse, she who not only has a great knowledge of her husband and her God, but who also enjoys His intimate friendship and familiarity, and merits to be often honoured by His embraces, and who even now inquires with such loving boldness where He reposes in the noonday, pasturing His happy flock. In this she desires, not to know Him whom she already knows, but to behold Him in His glory. And He thinks fit to reprove her on account of her presumption, and ignorance of herself, in imagining that she is capable of so great a vision, the excess of her love having caused her to forget that she is in a mortal body. She is convinced of her ignorance; she is rebuked for her temerity: "If you do not know yourself, go forth from my presence." The Lord thunders against his Beloved, not as Spouse but as Lord; not that He is in anger, but because He desires to purify her by fear, and to make her thus capable of the vision for which she sighs; this vision being the recompense of the pure in heart. Let her cease, then, so long as she is upon earth, to seek with too much curiosity that which is in heaven, lest, in searching for the secret of God, she should be overwhelmed with His glory. This vision, He says to her, is far above your powers. You are not yet strong enough to sustain the splendour of the noonday in which I dwell. This felicity is reserved for you in the end of time, when I shall present you to me clothed with glory, without stain or wrinkle, exempt from any fault. How can you, who are not yet all-beautiful, behold Him who is the source of all beauty?

The Song continues: "Your cheeks are beautiful as those of a dove." The Spouse is tenderly modest, and I believe that the reproof of her Lover has brought the colour into her face, and made her more lovely. In order to perceive the aptness of this comparison, remember that the intention is, as it were, the face of the soul; for the intention constitutes its rectitude, as the face is the beauty of the body. In the intention there are two things to be considered: the object and the cause; that is, what you propose, and why you propose it. When both are just and pure, the soul deserves that it should be said of her that her cheeks are beautiful. The cheeks of the Spouse are capable of different degrees of beauty, but then only are they perfectly beautiful when God is at once object and cause, and He is loved for Himself alone.

Why, however, is it said, "like those of a dove"? Because this bird is very chaste, spends her life with only one partner, and, losing that one, lives solitary. You, then, who, moved by the Holy Spirit, burn with desire to make your soul the Spouse of Jesus Christ, take care that both your cheeks are thus beautified. Forget your own people and the house of your father, and the King shall greatly desire your beauty. Holy Soul, remain in solitude, and keep yourself for Him who has chosen you from the others. You have a Lover who will not honour you with His presence when any other company is with you. This solitude should be all interior and of the soul, though solitude of the body likewise is often useful. You are interiorly alone if you are attached to nothing present, if you despise what many esteem, if you refuse what all desire, if you avoid contentions, if you do not feel losses, nor remember injuries. Otherwise you are not alone, even when you are alone. Thus, you see, you may be alone when you are with many, and with many when you are alone. In however numerous a company you find yourself, you are alone with God, if you do not listen curiously to anything that is said, and if you do not judge rashly. If you hear evil of any one, do not hasten to judge your neighbour, but excuse him if you can. Excuse the intention if you cannot the action. Think that he did it in ignorance, or by misfortune, or was surprised into doing it, or, at most, that perhaps the temptation was exceedingly strong; and say to yourself, What should I have done under like pressure?

"Your neck is like pearls." As by the cheeks the intention seems to be signified, so we may take the neck to mean the understanding. The understanding is, as it were, the neck by which the nourishment of the spirit, which is truth, passes into the soul, and diffuses itself into all her affections and activities. When the understanding is pure and simple, it shines like a pearl with the truth itself, and has no need of the external ornaments with which philosophers and unbelievers endeavour to hide the deformities of their intelligence.

"We will make you earrings of gold inlaid with silver." Here the companions of the Bride address her, promising her that, until she attains to that vision of her Lord the desire of which consumes her soul, they will comfort her with the precious informations of faith, "which comes by hearing," and purifies the eye, and prepares it for the vision of God. Gold inlaid with silver, means the celestial and ineffable good of heaven illustrated and made faintly intelligible by silver, which is the symbol of truth. These earrings, therefore, stand for the spiritual images and figures by which the soul assists herself in her contemplation of God, and in which she sees Him as in a glass darkly. These things are altogether Divine, and can be understood only by those who have had experience of them. These alone know how, in a mortal body and in the state of faith, it sometimes happens that the contemplation of pure truth begins already to outline its work in us, so that one who is so happy as to have received this gift from on high, can say with the Apostle: "I know in part;" and again: "We know in part, and we guess in part." When the soul, going as it were forth from itself, catches a momentary glimpse of that which is purely Divine, like a flash of lightning, it happens immediately—I know not whether in order to temper its splendour or to make us able to communicate it to others—that this apprehension accommodates itself to corporeal images and figures. These images I believe to be the work of our good Angels, as others which are evil are most certainly the doing of the ministers of evil.

We see that the Spouse has received quite another thing than she desired. She longed for the repose of contemplation; she receives instead wisdom with eloquence, which involves the obligation of laboriously propagating her knowledge. It was so with Jacob. He sought for the embraces of the beautiful but sterile Rachel, and received, in spite of himself, the fertile but weak-eyed Leah. Thus must God's Spouse often leave the kisses which are sweet, in order to give her breasts to His little ones. Woe to those who have received the grace of thoughts and words worthy of the greatness of God, if they make piety serve their own avarice, and turn into secret vainglory what they have received in order that they might win souls to God.

"My spikenard sent forth its odour." Spikenard is the humility with which the Spouse received her Lord's rebuke. Spikenard is a low-growing herb, which those who have studied the nature of simples say is of a warm nature. Such is the nature of that humility which glows with the ardour of divine love. There is one kind of humility which is produced by knowledge of the truth, but this is cold; there is another which is formed and inflamed by charity. One consists in knowledge, the other in the movements of the heart. If you look upon yourself in the light of truth and without dissimulation, I doubt not but that you will be humbled in your own eyes, though you may not have virtue enough to bear being humbled in those of others. This is to be humbled by means of truth, and not by the infusion of love. Those who love would wish—were it consistent with the good of others—to be thought of, by the whole world, as meanly as they think of themselves. They do not love the truth perfectly who do not desire that it should be known to all. Thus you see it is not by any means the same thing, to think of yourself without presumption and to be humble in heart. The first kind of humility is compulsory, the second voluntary. But our Lord says: "Learn of Me, for I am meek and humble of heart." Therefore, if you are become humble in your own eyes by the knowledge of the truth concerning yourself, take care that you add to this humility humility of heart. God abhors, as it is written, a double weight. Will you make yourself little in your own eyes, at the same time that you desire to be of much account in the eyes of others? This is to resist the truth and to fight against God.

But it is not much to have submitted one's self to God unless one is submitted to every creature for the love of God. If you will be perfect, make the first advance towards him who is less than you; defer to your inferior; respect him who is younger than you are. So will you be able to say with the Spouse: "My spikenard has sent forth its odour." This odour is love; the good impression which all persons will have of you; the good odour of Jesus Christ, admired by all, beloved by all. He whom truth alone humbles, cannot attain to this degree of perfection; his humility is for himself; it sends forth no odour, because it has none. The humility of the Spouse is voluntary, perpetual, and fertile; its odour is not diminished by reprimands nor by praises. The more she is exalted, the more she abases herself. She says: "God has regarded the lowliness of his handmaiden;" for what mean these words: "My spikenard has sent forth its odour," if not "My lowliness has been pleasing to God"?

"A little bunch of myrrh is my Beloved to me; He shall abide between my breasts." Just now she spoke of Him as the King, seated on high on His royal bed. But her humility has brought Him into her bosom. Myrrh, which is bitter, means tribulations. Seeing herself about to suffer for her Lover, she exults. "They went forth," says the Scripture, "rejoicing because they were accounted worthy to suffer for the name of Jesus." She calls the bunch of myrrh "little," because all that she can endure for His sake seems little. Little indeed; for the sufferings of this life are not to be compared with the glory which awaits her. That which is now a little bunch of myrrh shall one day be changed into a crown of glory and bliss. Observe that she does not say simply that "a little bunch of myrrh is my Beloved;" she adds, "to me," that is to me who love Him; for love makes great sacrifices little.

The bunch of myrrh between the breasts is also the memory of the Passion of Jesus Christ The breasts of the Spouse are congratulation and compassion, according to the doctrine of St. Paul, who bids us to rejoice with those that rejoice and to weep with them that weep; but in rejoicing and weeping there is danger of extremes, against which the bunch of myrrh, thus understood, will be the best safeguard. Say to yourself, O my soul, How many kings and prophets have desired to see what I see, and have not seen it! They have laboured, and I enjoy the fruits of their labours. I have gathered the myrrh which they planted. It shall remain for ever between my breasts. In meditating upon it lies the perfection of wisdom and goodness, the fulness of knowledge, the riches of salvation, the abundance of merit. It raises me in adversity, and controls me in prosperity; it enables me to walk in the royal road between the goods and evils of this life, and scatters the perils which threaten me from either side. In my mouth and in my heart is Jesus, and Jesus crucified. I will not inquire with the Spouse where He reposes at noonday whom I embrace with joy as he lies between my breasts. What she seeks is more exalted, but my satisfaction is more sweet and easy.

Dear children, prize this bunch of myrrh, and carry it always between your breasts. Always carry it where you can see it, for if you bear it without considering it, its weight will oppress you and its odour will not refresh you.

"Behold, thou art fair, my Love, behold thou art fair." This repetition is not without meaning. The soul has a double beauty. Her beauty is humility. "Sprinkle me with hyssop, and I shall be pure." This hyssop, which restores the soul's purity or beauty, is humility. But, although the humility of such as have fallen into great sin is lovely, it scarcely deserves a wondering praise. If, however, the soul which has preserved her innocence adds thereto humility, is she not doubly beautiful? The Blessed Virgin never lost her sanctity and never wanted humility; and, if the King greatly desired her beauty, it was because she joined lowliness to innocence. "He has regarded the lowliness of His handmaiden." Happy those who have kept their robes pure, that is to say, their simplicity and innocence, if, at the same time, they have been careful to clothe themselves with humility. To such it shall be said: "You are beautiful, my Love, you are beautiful." Dear Lord Jesus! may you be able to say to my soul, even once, that she is beautiful. I have ill kept my robe of baptism, but do Thou at least preserve in me humility!

"Our bed is covered with flowers. The beams of our house are of cedar, our rafters of cypress trees." You that hear these words of the Holy Spirit, do you recognise nothing in yourselves of the felicity of the Bride which is chanted in this canticle of love by that Spirit; or do you hear His voice, not knowing whence it cometh or whither it goeth? Perhaps you also desire the repose of contemplation which is herein spoken of. This desire is praiseworthy, if you do not forget the flowers of good works with which the Bride decks her bed. The exercise of virtues precedes this holy repose as flowers precede fruit. Think not to obtain this sweet rest of contemplation until you have earned it. Those who will not labour, as the Apostle says, shall not eat. "The keeping of Thy commandments has given me understanding," writes the Prophet, in order to teach us that the taste of contemplation only comes from the practice of obedience. In vain will you expect the visit of the Bridegroom if you have not prepared for Him a couch covered with the flowers of good works. How can you expect Him to give Himself to a rebel, who was Himself obedient unto death? Will He not rather say to you, in a voice of thunder: "I cannot abide your Sabbaths and your solemn feast days"?

I am astonished at the impudence of some among us, who, after troubling us with their singularity, impatience, obstinacy, and rebellion, dare to invite the Lord of all purity into souls thus stained. The Centurion, the perfume of whose sanctity is spread throughout Israel, besought Him not to enter into his house because of his unworthiness; the Prince of the Apostles cried: "Depart from me, O Lord, for I am a sinful man." But you say: "Come unto me, O Lord, for I am holy."

The beams of the house—which house you are, if you walk not after the flesh but the Spirit—must be of cedar, an incorruptible wood; lest, when you have begun to build, it should fall again to ruins. Let these beams be patience, for "the patience of the poor shall never perish;" longanimity, "for he who shall persevere to the end shall be saved;" but principally love, which "never fails" and "is stronger than death."

"The King brought me into the cellar of wine, he ordered love in me." The Spouse declares that she is inebriated with the King's love; for love is a strong wine. When the disciples were filled with the Holy Spirit the people said that they were drunk. They were so indeed, but it was with the Holy Ghost and not with wine. Was not the house in which they were assembled a great cellar of wine, and might not each of them say, as he went forth, inebriated with the affluence of the goods of that house, and satiated with the torrent of immortal delights: "The King brought me into the cellar of wine"?

If, in prayer, any one obtains the grace to be, as it were, ravished out of himself in the secret of the Divinity, and issues from that state on fire with the love of God, and inflamed with zeal for goodness and with a great fervour for all spiritual exercises, so that he can say, "My heart was hot within me, and while I was musing the fire kindled," manifestly he has been in the cellar of wine. In contemplation, there are two kinds of ecstasy, one of the spirit and the other of the heart. One consists in the enlightening of the understanding, the other in the ardour of the will; the one is knowledge, the other love; and every one who goes forth from his prayer filled with the abundance of these graces, is entitled to rejoice in the foregoing words of the Bride.

She adds: "He ordered love in me." It is very needful that it should be so; for what is there more insufferable than zeal without knowledge? The greater the zeal, the more is discretion necessary, that love may be ordered to its proper ends. Discretion orders all the virtues, and order produces grace, beauty, and stability. The prophet David says: "By Thine order the day goeth on;" the day means virtue, in which only the discreet persevere. Discretion, then, is not so much a special virtue, as the guide and moderator of all the virtues, regulating the affections and ordering the conduct of life. Without discretion nature degenerates into vice, and even natural love changes into passions which destroy nature.

Here it is fit that we should remember that there are two kinds of love. One consists in action, the other in affection. Active love is the proper subject of God's law; for who could love affectively in that degree of perfection which the First Commandment prescribes? Affective love is the recompense of active charity. There may be a commencement and some progress of affective love in this life, but the fulness of it constitutes the felicity to come. Or you may maintain, if it pleases you better, that God has commanded what is impossible, but that, in doing so, it is not to load us with inevitable sin, but to make us humble, and to show us that we cannot be saved by our righteousness but by His mere mercy. That the commandment, however, is directed to active rather than affective charity is manifest from our Lord's interpreting His own words,

"Love your enemies," by His immediately adding: "Do good to those that hate you;" and, as concerning the love which is directly due to Himself: "If you love me, keep My commandments."

I do not say that it can be well with us without affection, or that, with a cold and arid heart, it is sufficient only to bestir the hands of action. Among the catalogue of the greatest evils, enumerated by the Apostle, the want of affection is one. But there is an affection of the merely natural man, another of the rational mind, and a third which is the wisdom of love. The first, as the Apostle declares, is hostile to God, and cannot be made subject to Him in this life; the second is that which makes us consent to the will of God, because it is good; the third is a very different thing. It tastes with delight how sweet the Lord is; it excludes the first, and rewards the second. The first is pleasant, but sinful; the second dry, but strong; the third full of unction and blessedness. It is, then, the second which produces works, and it is real charity, loving not only "in deed" but "in truth," though not yet with the perceptible felicity of the highest kind of love. When the Bride says, "He ordered love in me," does she mean the active or affective charity? Both. But the order in the one is the reverse of the order in the other. Affective love always prefers God to man, and those among men who are most perfect to those who are less so. On the contrary, active love generally inverts this method. In helping our brethren we should be most assiduous with regard to those who have most need and are fullest of infirmities; we have to consider temporal before eternal things, though in ultimate view of them; it is often our duty to consider our bodily necessities before those of our soul; and altogether in this order the way is that "the last things shall be first, and the first last," and that we shall not consider the preciousness of things but the need of men.

But Wisdom, which is the embrace of Truth and Love, gives to all things their real value, delighting in God's supremacy, and in all others only in so far as they love Him and are like Him. One, so loving, recognises as his neighbour only him who loves God, and in proportion as he loves God. And, since he loves himself only as he loves God, he loves his neighbour as himself, no more nor less. As to his enemy, who if he does not love God is a mere nothing, it is impossible that he should love him as himself; but he loves him in order that he may come to love God, the possibility that he may do so rendering even him an object of some degree of affective charity.

"Sustain me with flowers, cover me with fruits; for I languish with love." The love of the Bride, we see, has been increased by the intimacies of her converse with her Lord, and she rejoices in His praises of her. "My soul," says the prophet, "shall be praised in the Lord: the humble shall hear thereof and be glad." She has come from drinking of their delights, but "they who drink me," as Wisdom declares, "shall still thirst." After all this happiness, the Bridegroom having absented Himself again, according to His custom, the Spouse cries that she languishes with love. The more delightful He makes His presence to her, so much the more grievous becomes His absence, and nothing augments desire for a beloved object so much as its loss. Therefore she asks to be refreshed by flowers and fruits until it shall please Him to return. Flowers mean faith, and fruits works. These are all that is left to the Soul, when, for a time, she loses the light of contemplation, which loss is continually happening to her, in order that she may desire her Lord more and more. At such times she can only console herself with good works proceeding from an unfeigned faith. Whenever she falls from contemplation, she retires into activity, as being the best means of recovering her repose. For action and contemplation are near relatives, and love to remain together. Martha is the sister of Mary, and when the Bride goes forth from the light of contemplation, it is not to fall into the darkness of sin or the negligence of sloth, but to sustain herself in the lesser light of good actions. Our Saviour's words, "Let your light shine before men," manifestly mean the light of deeds which men can see. "Sustain me with flowers, cover me with fruits; for I languish with love." When the beloved person is present, love is in its vigour; when absent, it languishes. This languor is a weariness and grief caused by the impatience of desire, which is necessarily very violent, in one that loves much, when the object of love is withdrawn. Therefore the Spouse earnestly asks that she may be able to refresh and repair her powers, while her Lord delays, with the fruits of good works and the cheering ardours of faith. I have experienced this myself. When I have seen that any of you, my children, have profited by my discourses, I do not repent of having preferred the trouble of teaching you to my spirit's repose. I do not regret to have interrupted the delightful exercise of contemplation, because I am surrounded by the flowers and fruits of piety. For it is long since that charity, "which seeks not its own," has persuaded me to care more for your advancement than for all else that is dearest to me. Praying, reading, writing, meditating, and all other spiritual exercises, I have counted but as loss for the love of you.

I remember to have given, in my book on the Love of God, a different sense to those words of the Bride which I have last explained. You who have read both will judge which is best. No discreet reader will blame me for having given two explanations of the same passage, so long as both are founded upon truth, and so long as charity, which is the rule for the interpretation of Scripture, edifies as many more persons as there are more who can be benefited by the two interpretations than by either one of them. Why should any person find it amiss that in the use of Scripture we should do otherwise than we do daily in many things? To how many uses do we put water, for example? Thus we are not to be blamed who find divers senses in one and the same Word of God, provided that they serve divers needs of the soul.

The Song continues: "His left hand is under my head, and with His right hand he will embrace me." It seems that the Bridegroom is returned, to recreate with His presence His Spouse, who languished with love. For He can never delay long when He is called with such ardent desires. And, as He finds that, during His absence, she has been faithfully labouring to amass riches of good works, He returns to her with more abundant graces than before. Happy the soul which reposes on the bosom of the Lord, and rests between His arms. "His left hand is under my head, and with His right He will embrace me." She does not say: "He embraces me," but, "He will embrace me," in order to show that she is so thankful for the first favour that she anticipates even the second with acts of grace. Learn from this not to be slothful and a laggard in giving thanks. The wise man bids us to consider with care every gift of God, that we may let none, great or small, pass without answering gratitude. Our Lord bids us gather the least remains, so that nothing may be lost; that is to say, that we must not forget His least benefits. For is not everything lost which is given where there is no gratitude? Ingratitude is the enemy of the soul, the annihilation of merit, the dissipation of virtue, and the loss of all the favours which God does us. It is a burning wind which dries up the source of goodness, the dews of pity, the rivers of grace. As I have elsewhere explained, at large, the meaning of the left hand and the right, I will go on to the next words.

"I adjure you, O ye daughters of Jerusalem, that ye wake not my Beloved till she pleases." These daughters of Jerusalem are the actions and affections which, though good in themselves, are disturbers of the higher good, the sleep of the soul in contemplation. This sleep is dear to God, and He Himself watches over it. There are some among us who are so happy as to have experienced this mystery, so full of joy; this watching of God over the blissful repose of His Spouse, in which He protects that repose, which no words can describe, from all interruptions, until she herself shall please to recur to her ordinary activities. This sleep is a kind of death which is the life of the Soul. "You are dead, and your life is hidden with Jesus Christ in God." The Soul, thus gone forth from herself, glides safely among the snares and pitfalls of this life, without as much as being aware of them. How shall she fear the delusions of the senses, whose senses are killed by the sense of God? Happy death, the death of the just, which destroys not life, but betters it; which does not smite down the body, yet exalts the spirit. But this death, which is death to temptation, is, thus far, only the death of the righteous. May I die the death of the angels, for this is indeed contemplation, the God-guarded sleep of the Beloved! May I be sometimes able, not only to lose the love of things present, but the very apprehension of them, commercing only with those whose purity I would imitate! In this life, to live untouched by the love of the things of this life is after all no more than human virtue; but not to be turned from contemplation by the images of the senses is a truly angelic purity. In the first case, indeed, you go forth from yourself, but only to remain near to yourself; but, in the latter, you go far as well as forth from yourself. Until you are able to raise yourself, by the purity of your spirit, above all the phantoms of corporeal things, do not expect to attain to this repose. The secret of solitude, the serenity of light, the abode of peace, is not below you, that is to say, is not in anything which imagination can represent to you.

The daughters of Jerusalem are entreated by the Bridegroom not to awake the Beloved from her sleep "till she pleases." This implies a permission to the soul to be her own director in the division of her time between the different duties of Martha and Mary. If she loves so much as to be capable of true contemplation, there is no fear that she will neglect the many services of charity, though she will always avoid being busied in them. The Spouse, delighted with the assurance that she cannot do better than indulge as she will in the delightful leisure, or rather say, the ardent exercise of contemplation, exclaims with rapture: "It is the voice of my Beloved!" This happy assurance is especially necessary to quiet the scruples of the contemplative who has the welfare of others in charge. He is often fearful lest he should be caring more for his own good than theirs, and it is no small consolation when he is able to read God's approval of his ways in the strength and sweetness with which he finds by experience that his external activity is invested by them.

"Behold, He standeth behind our wall, looking through the windows, looking through the lattices." The wall is the flesh, and the approach of the Divine Lover, the Incarnation. The lattices and the windows are the senses and passions of humanity which He assumed, in order that, looking upon us through them, He might have compassion on us.

"Behold, my Beloved speaketh to me." Remark how carefully the Spouse observes everything that her Beloved does with regard to her. "He is come," "He hastens," "He approaches," "He arrives," "He looks," "He speaks." He comes in the Angels, He hastens in the Patriarchs, He approaches in the Prophets, He is present in the flesh, He looks on us in miracles, He speaks in the Apostles. Or, otherwise, He comes by prevenient grace, He hastens by the zeal of His love for us, He approaches by humbling Himself, He is present to those who present themselves to Him, He looks on the predestined, He speaks in teaching or inspiring the doctrines of the Kingdom of God. I would that the task of teaching you all this was not mine. Good men love to keep silence concerning that which they have learned in silence; they find it best to hide the secret of the King in their own bosoms. But, since these will not speak, I must, for my office bids me preach. If, then, I am warned, either from without by man, or from within by the Holy Spirit, to keep justice and equity, I regard this as a messenger of the coming of the Spouse, bidding me make ready to receive Him. For it is written: "Justice shall go before Him;" "By justice and equity is Thy throne prepared;" "Sanctity becomes well the house of the Lord;" "His place is in peace;" "The pure in heart shall see God." The reprimands and exhortations of the just are words yet more pressing. If these take effect in you, and, being received without repugnance, nay, with pleasure and ardour, then the Lover of your soul not only comes, but hastens; for, if you hasten to receive His words, it is because He first hastens to enter into you; for "in this is love, not as though we had loved God, but because He hath first loved us." If you are heated by His word, if it burns you with compunction for your sins, remember that "a fire shall go before Him," and be sure that He is then very near. "He is nigh to those that are of a contrite heart." But if it converts you wholly to Him, if it causes you to come to an effectual determination to keep all His commandments; above all, if you feel yourselves on fire with His love, then be sure that He, who is a consuming fire, is Himself present in you, burning up the evil in you, and changing your substance into His own. But, consuming fire as He is, He burns sweetly and destroys happily, and is at once blasting and unction. When this fire in you has consumed the filth of sin and the stains of your vices, and purified and calmed your conscience, you experience a sudden and extraordinary expansion of the heart and an infusion of light, and you are able to understand the Scriptures and to penetrate the mysteries of faith. This is the effect of a look of the Bridegroom, who thus makes your righteousness to shine as the noonday. But, so long as the ruinous walls of the body are standing, this light is only seen through cracks and crevices. As the great Contemplative writes: "We see now as in a glass darkly, but hereafter face to face." After the splendour of this glance of the Divine Lover, so full of goodness and compassion, comes His voice, which softly and sweetly insinuates His holy will. This voice is love itself; it cannot be idle; it is incessantly solicitous of good. It says: "Arise, make haste," and bids the Spouse endeavour to win others to seek a like happiness. For it is the property of true contemplation to inflame the soul with so great a desire for the same blessedness in others, that she often willingly abandons contemplation for the labour of teaching. She then returns to her own joy with double ardour, the fruit of her good works; but only to go forth again with increased vigour to similar labours. These recurrent alternations are not without distress. She is fearful of attaching herself too much to either state, trembling lest she fail in the least in aught that God requires of her. She complains, with holy Job: "When I lie down to sleep, I say, When shall I arise, and when I am risen, I wait impatiently for night." That is, when I am in my repose I accuse myself of having neglected work, and when I am at work I blame myself for having troubled my repose.

The Bridegroom accompanies this injunction to arise and make haste with renewed praises of the beauty of the Spouse; and every soul may rejoice in being thus reputed perfect by her Lord, if, like this Spouse, she sighs over her own shortcomings, rejoices in God, and does good to her neighbour.

You remember that the Bridegroom just now bade the daughters of Jerusalem, the activities of external life, not to awake the Spouse "till she please;" and now He Himself bids her to "arise and make haste, and come." It is a different thing for the daughters of Jerusalem to disturb her, and for the Lord she loves, and on whose bosom she is resting, to bid her arise and come, that is, come with Him. For this His bidding is also the injunction of her own heart, which is one with His. To be bidden by Him is to be drawn by Him, and nothing is difficult or unpleasant in His company. "Be Thou with me," says Job, "and let who will be against me;" and David: "Though I walk through the valley of the shadow of death, I will fear nothing; for Thou art with me."

"Winter is now past, the rain is over and gone, the flowers have appeared in our land, the time of pruning is come." Winter is that fear which is indeed the beginning of wisdom, but which is as yet unaccompanied by love. Love, the state of perfection, is the summer of the soul. It dries up the wintry rains, that is, the bitter tears caused by former sins and by the dread of the judgment of God. The summer has also rains, but they are soft and fertilising. What is more sweet than the tears of love? Love weeps for desire; it weeps for sympathy; but not for grief. The time is come for pruning the vine. That is the great work which remains to be done. Let us examine then our ways, and let every one reckon that he is advanced, not in so far as he finds nothing in himself to correct, but as love makes him quick to discover and diligent to amend all that is amiss. For who is so perfect that he can find no branch of his vine that wants pruning? The evil which is cut off, buds and grows again, the vice which has been chased away returns, the fire which has been subdued revives. It is not enough to have pruned once; we must prune often, nay, always. As long as you are in this mortal body, the Jebusite will always inhabit your land. He may be subjugated, but never exterminated.

"The voice of the turtle is heard in our land." It is the Bridegroom that speaks, and He says "our land." Think how sweet it is to hear the God of Heaven say "in our land," that is, in our earth. O children of men, inhabitants of earth, the Lord has indeed done great things for you! Wonderful is His commerce with earth, wonderful His relations to the Spouse, whom He has been pleased to create from earth in order to unite Himself with her most intimately. This word is not a word of sovereignty, but of familiar alliance. It is the word, not of a Lord, but a Husband. "Thy Maker is thy Husband;" "He that created me has rested in my tabernacle." He is our Creator, and He makes Himself our most intimate companion. It is not wonderful, for it is love that speaks, and love knows no inequality. He is not only one among us but one of us, and our earth is not only His possession but His own country. And well it may be so, for from earth comes His Spouse, and He has made Himself one flesh with her. If they have but one flesh, why should they not have one country?

"Catch us the little foxes that destroy the vines." The vines are the souls of those who have become spiritual. Foxes are temptations. There must needs be temptations; for who shall be crowned unless he has lawfully combated? And how shall he combat if he is never attacked? When, therefore, you enter on the service of God, hold yourselves firmly in His fear, and prepare your souls for temptation, assured that all who will live holily in Jesus Christ must suffer persecution. Now, the nature of temptation varies greatly according to the advance which has been made. For beginners, who are as the tender flowers of early spring, it is the violence of frost that is most to be feared. But those who are more advanced have not to fear open enemies, but artful foxes; secret evils which have the semblance of virtues. How many have I known, who, having gone on to a fair degree of perfection, have at last found themselves shamefully and miserably ruined by the wiles of these foxes! How many, for example, have fallen from their duty to God and to themselves in their anxiety to teach or otherwise benefit others, before they were called upon to do so, forgetting that the function of a penitent is not to preach, but to weep. How many have fallen through indiscreet austerities, and other religious irregularities.

"My Beloved to me, and I to Him." This word seems simple, for it is sweet, but it is full of mysteries which none but the holy can savour. It is love that speaks, and not the understanding. It is rather breathing than speaking, and it is breathing one breath with her Beloved, with whom, indeed, she has become one spirit. We do not require clearness in such language. It is like a precious prefume. Such perfumes are the effusions of St. John, the odours of the eternity, the generation and the divinity of the Word. What a good odour of Jesus Christ have not the sayings of St. Paul diffused throughout the world! He does not utter, indeed, the ineffable words which it was given to him to hear; but with what ardour of desire does he make me feel what I am not yet allowed to understand! I know not how it is, but the more the realities of heaven are clothed with obscurity, the more they delight and attract, and nothing so much heightens longing as such tender refusal. "My Beloved to me, and I to Him." We can see, at least, in these words an ardent and reciprocal love of two persons, one for the other. They reveal the felicity of the one and the marvellous bounty of the other. But who will dare to flatter himself that he understands what is received and given in this interchange of exceeding love, unless, by a singular purity of body and soul, he has merited to experience something of this sort in himself? For all this is a movement of the heart, and the understanding knows nothing of it. How few are they who can boast that, "Beholding the glory of the Lord with open face, they are transformed into the same image from glory to glory, as by the spirit of the Lord." And yet no others can read aright these words of the Spouse.

There are, however, in these words, certain meanings of which our gross and common apprehensions are capable. They include an assertion of grace prevenient as the source and condition of the subsequent and co-operating grace in the soul. "I to Him" because He is "first to me." I am able to look upon Him because He has looked upon me. The soul, which is truly the Spouse of God, perceives that she has received both graces. They include, also, the assertion of an especial regard or attention of either person towards the other. Notwithstanding the immense distance between God and the Soul, He regards her, and the Church, which is nothing else but her multiplied perfection, as necessary to His own perfection. "All things are for the Elect;" hence nothing is complete without the Elect. The Spouse speaks so boldly concerning her Lord's regard, because she knows that He has need of her. All His works remain unfinished until her perfection is fulfilled. "All creation groans together, waiting for the revelation of the sons of God." The glory of the angels is defective, and the city of God wants its integrity, wanting the perfection of her who was made a little lower than the angels in order that she might be its crowning glory and honour. The joy of those who have once suffered is a joy which Heaven can only know in the persons of, and by sympathy with, the children of the Church. Those who have always rejoiced can have no such joy as this. It is truly joy when joy succeeds to sorrow, rest to labour, and the harbour to the storm. To have passed from death to life is life indeed. This, in the celestial banquet, shall be my peculiar dainty; and I will venture to say that the angels themselves would not be wholly happy unless, by charity, they could enjoy this blessedness in me, and for my sake. We can see well, therefore, why there should be more joy in heaven over one repentant sinner than over ninety and nine just that need no repentance. And, if my tears make the delight of angels, what shall be my own delight! All their occupation is to praise God, but His praise is imperfect if there are none to cry: "We have passed through fire and water, and Thou hast brought us into a place of refreshment."

From this we may understand that we need not trouble ourselves concerning the disproportion of our merits and God's promises. We see that He has made us and our felicity, not for us, but for Himself, and we merit enough in this matter if we confess that our merits have nothing to do with it. Nevertheless, though our merits do not obtain for us this felicity, without merits none shall possess it. Pray, therefore, equally against indigence of merit and presumption of desert, as the Wise Man meant to do when he said: "Give me neither riches nor poverty."

It is clear that all the words and praises of the Spouse in this Song are true of the Church, but it is not so clear how far each soul in grace may apply such things to herself. There are spiritual persons who serve God, not only with fidelity, but with confidence, and who have a right to address Him as a friend, their conscience bearing witness in them that He is well pleased that they should do so. Who are these persons? God only knows. But hear how it must be with you, if you would be of their number. And now I do not speak from experience, but from a desire to experience. Give me a soul who loves nothing but God, or whatever she ought to love for His sake; who not only lives in Jesus Christ, but has long done so; who has no other study or pleasure than to have God always before her eyes, and who will not and cannot occupy herself with any other than her Lord. I will not deny that such a soul is worthy of such regards and attentions from her Master, and, if it pleases her to boast of them, I see no reason why she should not do so, so long as she makes her boast of herself in the Lord. "My soul shall be praised in the Lord; the humble shall hear thereof and be glad."

The holy soul may derive a great confidence in the individual love of the Bridegroom from a consideration of the great simplicity of His nature, which enables Him to regard many as one and one as many, without being Himself multiplied by multitude nor diminished by singularity, nor divided by diversity of objects, nor constrained by their likeness; so that He can belong utterly to one without being absorbed or prevented from belonging equally to many; and belong to many in such manner that He gives His whole heart to one.

The bounty of the Word and the good will of the Father are so great towards a well-natured and well-ordered soul, that her, whom they have thus by grace prevented and prepared (which is the gift of the Father and the work of the Son), they deign so to honour with their presence, that they not only visit her, but establish themselves in her as their abode (John 14:23). They are not satisfied with manifesting themselves to her; they give themselves to her. The coming of the Son into the Soul is the entry of the truth; the coming of the Father is when the Soul is so touched with the love of the truth that she is able to say: "I am in love with His beauty."

When I find that my spirit is open to the intelligence of Holy Writ, when the words of wisdom flow abundantly from my heart, when mysteries are revealed to me by an infusion of light from on high, when heaven opens above me, and diffuses in my soul the fertile rains of meditation, I cannot doubt that the Husband of my soul is present. For these riches come from the Word, of whose fulness we receive. If, in addition, I feel myself penetrated with the dews and unction of a humble and devout zeal, so that the love of the known truth engenders in me hatred and contempt of all vanity, and prevents knowledge from puffing me up and the visits of God from elating me; then I recognise with certainty the effect of the paternal tenderness, and I know that my Father is with me. But if I persevere in corresponding, as far as I am able, with so great a goodness, by movements and acts in some degree proportioned thereto, and if I find that the grace of God is not in vain in me, then I am assured that the Father and the Son have taken up their abode in me, the one nourishing and the other instructing. I think that such a Soul may say, without fear, "My Beloved to me;" since, perceiving that she loves God, and that she loves Him with ardour, she cannot doubt that she is passionately loved by Him; and by the fixed intention, diligence, care, watchfulness, and zeal, with which she incessantly seeks the means of pleasing Him, she knows certainly that the movements of love are from and in Him, and she remembers this promise: "With the measure with which thou metest it shall be measured again to thee." She knows, indeed, that she loves Him only because He first loved her, but having been thus capacitated for looking upon Him she applies herself to regard Him continually, and becomes changed from glory to glory, and transformed into His image by beholding Him. He says: "I love them that love me, and they who seek me early in the morning shall find me." If you watch, He watches; rise before dawn to meet Him, you will find Him, but you will not be there before Him. He still prevents you with His grace. He loves you more than you love Him, and He loved you before you loved Him. I will add, for the understanding of spiritual persons, this seemingly astonishing yet most real thing, that, to the Soul who sees God, He makes as if He saw nothing but her, He applies Himself to her as if there existed nothing else, and she to Him, for she also can see nothing else. And what is this but for the Soul really and actually to be the wife and to be treated as the wife of God?

"My Beloved to me, and I to Him, who feedeth among the lilies." The lilies are the Soul's beauties, her virtues. Of these, truth, meekness, and justice are the principal. Truth is an excellent lily, odorous and having the splendour of the eternal light. Meekness has the whiteness of innocence and the perfume of hope, and shines with the duties of charity. Justice is also a choice lily, and its odour reaches even to the unjust, for it is "to one indeed the odour of death unto death; but to the other the odour of life unto life." Innocence and continence, or the power of controlling all concupiscences, are two lilies which are always found wherever the Beloved feeds, and, if to these two only, we add patience in temptations, His presence will be certainly secured.

Immediately after the last words, the Bride cries: "Return!" How shall I explain the mysterious reasons of these changes, these goings and returnings of the Divine Bridegroom? When the Soul is sensible of grace, she knows that the Beloved is present with her; when it is withdrawn, she complains that He is absent; and this invitation to return is the inevitable cry of the heart which has once known His pleasantness. Show me now a soul whom the Divine Word is accustomed to visit often, a soul to whom familiarity has given boldness, the taste of His sweetness, hunger, and a contempt for all else, peace, and I will show you the Spouse who speaks thus. She is bold with knowledge that she merits His presence, for otherwise she would call, not recall, Him. He comes and goes in this Soul at His good pleasure. He alone knows the season and the reason. We may be sure, indeed, that His purpose is to increase the love of His Spouse for Him, but the immediate cause of each visit or withdrawal is hidden.

"His footsteps are not known." "A little while, and you shall not see me; and again a little while, and you shall see me." A little while! Ah, dear Lord, how long that little while is! The time of Thine absence is short, indeed, if we consider our deservings, but very long to our desires. But the soul that loves is carried away by the ardour of the latter; she forgets her little merits and the majesty of her Lord. She thinks of nothing but her delights in His health-giving grace, and behaves familiarly with Him, recalling Him without fear or shyness, and demanding with confidence the restoration of her former pleasures. She does not call Him, "Lord" but "Beloved," "Return, my Beloved."

His coming and going are known only by their effects. His ways are past finding out, but His presence is living and efficacious. He awakens the Soul from her sleep; He agitates, softens, and pierces the heart, which before was sick, and as hard as stone. He roots up, destroys, edifies, and plants, waters what was dry, illuminates what was dark, expands what was narrow, inflames what was cold, makes straight what was crooked, and easy what was rough; so that we "bless the Lord, and all that is within us glorifies His holy name."

The visits of the Divine Lover are full of grace and truth. His presence is imperfect when either is lacking. The severity of the truth is painful without the gladness of grace, and the gladness of grace seems somewhat too free without the gravity of truth. Truth is bitter when unseasoned with the grace of devotion, and the fervour of devotion is apt to be too light, immoderate and uncontrolled, if not held back by the curb of truth. How many have received grace in vain, because they have not at the same time received the tempering of truth! They have indulged too much in the complacency of devotion; they have not attended enough to the warning regards of truth. Thus they have lost the grace to which they have addicted themselves with too partial an attachment, forgetting to "serve God with fear, and to rejoice in Him with trembling." One suffices not without the other; nay, one is not even good without the other. The Apostle charges them with a double guilt who know the truth, but have not grace to do it. On the other hand, it is written that "when Judas had swallowed the morsel which Jesus gave him, Satan entered into him." Many have been fed with the fine flower of wheat and with honey out of the stony rock, who have been all the more the enemies of God. Having but one foot to walk on, they have halted in their ways. The punishment of those who walk only by grace will be that of him who was a liar from the beginning, and of whom it is said: "Thou hast lost thy wisdom through thy beauty." Do you ask me, What is this dangerous and harmful beauty? It is your own. It is not said that Lucifer lost wisdom through beauty, but through his beauty. Now the beauty of the soul as well as that of the angel is wisdom, for, without it, what are they but unformed substances? But the angel lost it when he appropriated it to himself, and, with it, he lost his beauty. He did not give the glory to God; he did not render grace for grace; and so did not possess it according to the truth. The foolish virgins are those who believe their wisdom to be theirs, and they shall hear the terrible words: "I do not know you." And those who glorify themselves on account of extraordinary grace shall bear the same condemnation. Therefore let those tremble more than others who receive greater favours.

"In my little bed by night I have sought Him whom my soul loveth." Why has she recalled Him in vain? In order that her desire might be augmented, her affections proved, and her love inflamed. His absence is in dissimulation, not in anger. She seeks Him first in her little bed, that is, in the repose of contemplation, in her own bosom. Not finding Him, she goes forth into the streets and public places; but she finds Him neither in repose nor action. He will be found in His own time. "Seek and ye shall find;" but not in the night, in which it is said that the Spouse seeks Him. He is Himself the day, and at His coming she shall find Him.

"Have you not seen Him whom my soul loveth?" O violent, burning, impetuous love, which considers nothing but itself, despises all else, and finds itself all-sufficient! It confounds order, cares nought for custom, ignores measure, triumphing in itself over all rules of fitness, reason, decorum, prudence, and judgment. The words of the Bride are nothing else but this love: "Have you not seen Him whom my soul loveth?" As if they knew her thoughts, as if they knew His name! "What are you, and who is He?" In this singular negligence of words, this part of Scripture differs from all others. But, in this Epithalamium, as I said before, we must not consider words, but affections. Love speaks all through it, and, if you wish to understand it, you must love. To such as do not love it is a strange and barbarous tongue.

Having found Him again, the Spouse says: "I will hold Him; I will not let Him go." Perhaps He desires as much to be held fast by her as she desires to hold Him so; for does He not say: "My delights are to be with the children of men"? And has He not promised: "I will be always with you to the consummation of the ages"? What can be stronger than this mutual bond, which is sealed by the will and the reciprocal desire of both? She holds Him, but He holds her. "Thou hast held me by my right hand." She holds Him by the firmness of her faith and the ardour of her zeal. But she could not hold Him long unless He also held her.

Here I will pause to consider upon what grounds the Soul lays claim to all this astonishing familiarity and as it were equality in love. It is that she has been made after the image and in the likeness of God. The greatness of this character she has not lost by sin, though she has lost its rectitude. She is still a capacity for the Infinite. Filled as she is with vices, bound round with sin as with nets, seduced by pleasure, in banishment, shut up in her body as in a prison, sunk in the mud of her impurities, borne down with cares, absorbed by earthly thoughts, smitten with fears, oppressed by sorrows, misled by error, gnawed by weariness, full of suspicion, a stranger in the land of her enemies, she is still, I say, though so desperate and so damned, able to find in herself, not only the hope of pardon and pity, but that which justifies her in daring to aspire to the celestial nuptials of the Word, to the contraction of a most intimate alliance with God, and to the bearing of the blessed yoke of love with the King of angels. What may she not dare to undertake in confidence with regard to Him of whom she is still the image, and whose likeness she still bears? How should she fear His majesty when she considers the nobility of her own origin? All she has to do is to preserve the renewed purity of her nature in the decorum of her life, and to adorn and embellish, by virtues and good works, that illustrious image which is indelibly stamped in her creation.

Why does she remain idle and unserviceable? She is capable of labour and industry. They are gifts of nature; but if she does not use them, all her good inclinations will be lost in sleep and lethargy. They are the means by which she can rise, if she will; for God always keeps alive in her some spark of virtue and generosity, in order that she may be incessantly warned, by this her likeness to Him, either to remain with Him, or to return if she has quitted Him. She quits Him, not by removing from one place to another, but, after the manner of spiritual substances, by her corrupt affections, and the disorder of her life and conduct, causing her to degenerate from her native dignity, and to become unlike herself. This unlikeness, however, is not extinction, but a vice of her nature, and she returns when she turns herself towards the Word, in order to be reformed by and conformed with Him.

It is this conformity which makes a marriage between the Soul and the Word, when, being like Him by nature, she endeavours to resemble Him in will, loving Him as He loves her. If she loves perfectly, she becomes His Spouse. What can there be more delightful than this conformity, what more desirable than this love, which, not content with the instructions which she receives from men, boldly approaches the Word in her own person, attaches herself firmly to Him, interrogates and consults Him familiarly about all things, the capacity of her understanding being the only measure of the hardihood of her desires? This is a true marriage-contract; nay, more, it is a real embrace; for the complete conjunction of their wills makes one spirit of them. Nor need it be apprehended that the inequality of persons can render this union defective. Love knows nothing about respectful fear. Love consists in loving, not honouring. Astonishment, fear, wonder, are good for those to whom they are seasonable. The lover knows nothing of them. Love is full of itself. When love is born in the soul it absorbs all other passions. She that loves, loves, and ignores everything; and He who deserves to be honoured, feared, and admired, loves still better to be loved. Behold here a husband and a wife! For what is the essential of wedlock but to love and be loved?

Consider, further, that, in this case, the Bridegroom is not only a Lover, He is Love. Is He not also Honour? Let who will maintain it; I have never read it; but I have read that "God is Love." Not that God does not desire to be honoured, for He says: "If I am a Father, where is my honour?" But, so speaking, He speaks as a Father. As Husband of the soul, He says: "If I am a Husband, where is the love due to Me?" As Lord, also, He requires fear. Fear as Lord, honour as Father, love as Husband. But of these three which is best? Surely it is love. Lacking love, fear is painful, honour without reward. Fear is servile if unenfranchised by love, and honour which does not spring from love is flattery. Honour and fear are indeed God's due, but He will accept neither one nor the other unless they are seasoned with the honey of love. Whereas love is all-sufficient by itself. Love is its own merit and its own recompense. It seeks no reason nor gain out of itself. I love because I love; I love for the sake of loving. Love is a great thing, when, making its source its object, it renews there its streams in ever-increasing bounty. Of all the movements of the Soul, love is the only one which gives her Creator like for like. If He is angry with me, I do not reply with anger, but with self-abasement; if He rebukes me, I do not rebuke Him, but I confess His justice; if He commands, I answer with obedience; if He loves, on the contrary, it is that I may reciprocate His love, and that, and that only, is what He requires of me.

Love, as I have said, is a great thing; but it has degrees. That of the Spouse is the highest. Children love, but they think of the inheritance, and, fearing to lose it, they feel more respect than love. The whole good and only hope of the Spouse is love: and, if she loves abundantly, her Lover is content. She can give Him nothing more. This singleness of love is peculiar to marriage, and is found in no other relationship. He is Love, she is the Spouse of Love, and she is the only one who loves for love's sake only.

And with good reason it is that, renouncing every other thought, she gives herself wholly to love, since, by a reciprocal love, she is able to discern Him who is Love itself. For, should she wholly dissolve into love, what would she be in comparison with that inexhaustible fountain-head of love? The waters of the Lover and the Beloved, of the Soul and the Word, of the Bride and the Bridegroom, of the Creator and the creature, of her who thirsts and of Him who assuages thirst, do not flow with the same abundance. But what then? Shall the prayers of the Spouse, her desires, her ardour, her trust,—shall they be lost because she cannot run with a giant, dispute sweetness with honey, mildness with the lamb, whiteness with the lily, splendour with the sun, love with Him who is Love? Assuredly not; for, though the creature loves less than He by whom she is loved, yet, if she loves with all her power, her love is without defect. All for all is an equal bargain. It is therefore that I said that to love thus is to contract marriage with God; for it is impossible to love thus and to be little loved in return. Verily she is prevented and surpassed in love. Happy she who has deserved to be prevented with the benediction of so great a sweetness! Happy she who enjoys those chaste and sacred embraces of a love holy and pure, delightful and pleasant, calm and sincere, mutual, intimate, and violent, which joins two persons in one! For "They who love God are one Spirit with Him."

# THREE ROSARIES OF OUR LADY BY MARIANNE CAROLINE PATMORE

## A ROSARY IN HONOUR OF OUR LADY AS CO-REDEMPTRIX

A ROSARY in honour of OUR LADY as Co-Redemptrix—dwelling on the self-sacrifice, the union of the heart with God, the sharing of her Son's humiliation, the conquest of self-love and maternal love, out of conformity with the will of God, Godlike desire for the salvation of souls, and zeal for God's glory, in Mary as the perfect creature.

---

### FIRST JOYFUL MYSTERY

### THE ANNUNCIATION OF OUR LADY

MARY was alone; pure, simple, happy, in God, when the Archangel came to offer her the desire of every maiden of her race.

In that supreme hour she might have been perturbed by a delight too ecstatic for a mortal heart; but she was stilled by the high necessity of embracing with it a like lot to her Son's, a suffering as transcendent as her joy. She knew why God would put on flesh; she knew that He, our Life (who as God hath life in Himself), came to take from His mother a mortal life, the power to die. Could her heart endure to crucify itself by giving up her child to insult, suffering, and death? Mary alone of all creatures could have done it, because she alone had been created and fitted for this end. She said, "Behold the handmaid of the Lord; be it done to me according to Thy word;" and in lowly love and perfect stillness she received the coming of God.

Son of Mary, conceived by the Holy Ghost, have mercy and hear our prayer....

Mary, overshadowed by the power of the Most High, pray for us.

## SECOND JOYFUL MYSTERY

## THE VISITATION OF OUR LADY

MARY arose with haste. She hurried to her cousin's house. She yearned to carry the miracle within her, where the divine power was already miraculously at work. Did she know that the forerunner would adore his Lord? Did she only guess that where God was so present in blessing and in chastisement, her Babe and she would be acknowledged? or did she crave a refuge for a little in the hills to ponder on what now she knew, before she should begin her martyrdom by facing silently the alarm of tender, holy Joseph? Her heart, even her heart, was full to bursting. No word of hers was to tell her husband of her high calling and his own. As yet she was even to go through the piteous agony of his suspicion. And yet her heart was full of ecstasy.

In the house of the speechless Zachary, the unborn, speechless infant leapt for joy at the sound of her voice, and his aged mother proclaimed the dignity of Mary, and abased herself before the mother of her Lord.

Well had our Lady come here by Holy Ghost, for here she freely may break forth, "My soul doth magnify the Lord, and my spirit hath rejoiced in God my Saviour." Once only in all her life (for us), this once, the Alleluia of her heart must ring out. The first Christian hymn is this of Mary; the expression of the divinest joy mortal can ever know; good for every Christian when, in Holy Communion, God comes to enter into him. We are not only unworthy (that was Mary), we are degraded and defiled; yet that divine indwelling is vouchsafed also to us, and though no other mortal love, or sacrifice, can ever equal hers, each heart can try to make his own our Lady's song of joy.

Holy God, Holy and Strong, Holy and Immortal, inhabiting the Immaculate, of Thy mercy grant our prayer....

Virgin Mary, Mother of God, pray to Jesus for us.

## THIRD JOYFUL MYSTERY

## THE BIRTH OF OUR SAVIOUR CHRIST IN BETHLEHEM

FROM the coming of the Holy Ghost, Mary had been rapturously conscious that she was God's living temple; that hidden in her body, taking form from her substance, was He whom the heaven of heavens cannot contain, whom she had adored and served; but whom now she worshipped with a passionate love of union and possession. In her, the Infinite was small. In her, God had assumed not only the features of humanity but her own, the likeness of His mother. As her expectation neared its term, Mary longed for the hour when He should manifest Himself. Surrounded by the heavenly court (unseen, unheard, adoring), she waited God's mysterious pleasure. Yet she would fain have never let Him go. It was the beginning of their parting. And when the Desire of all nations, the well-beloved, co-equal Son, lay in her arms, so small and weak and helpless, how Mary longed that her sole worship by its wholeness and its ardour might make up to Him for the ignorance, indifference, and hatred of the world. She heard the angels' song; she saw the shepherds' adoration and the wise men's worship; she knew the love and reverence of Joseph, but she, the humblest of all creatures, knew that no created adoration could approach her own; for He that is mighty had done for her great things. He had kept her immaculate, He had taken her to be His Bride, and that flesh in which the Word of God was clothed, He had accepted of her substance.

O Babe in swaddling clothes, Emmanuel, our King and Lawgiver, the Saviour, have mercy on us, grant our prayer....

Mother, sweetest, pray for us.

## FOURTH JOYFUL MYSTERY

### THE PRESENTATION OF OUR BLESSED SAVIOUR IN THE TEMPLE

IN this mystery we have Mary's ceremonial profession of self-sacrifice. She went to the temple humbly imitating her Son. Though He was equal with the Father, He "emptied Himself" for our salvation, and through Mary He became "obedient unto death." Though she was the immaculate Bride of the Father, and Mother of God the Son, she consented to hide her blessedness, and carried her divine Babe to the temple with the typical price of redemption. She was humble not only for herself, but for Him. She made as if He were the child of Joseph; and she (Virgin of virgins) a woman needing the sacrifice of purification. But her humility was met by God's love. Her Infant was hailed and adored as our Salvation, the Light and Glory of the world; and she was associated in the very temple with Jesus in the anguish He had come to suffer, and the work He had come to do: "thine own soul a sword shall pierce." And Mary did not flinch. She stood fast in faith and love and lowliness; the cost well counted. She had been counting it ever since that day when she was made doubly unlike all women, by the coming of the Holy Ghost, that she might conceive the Redeemer. She offered Jesus unto God. She offered her own heart as well; she pledged herself to refuse God nothing; to be content to see the Son of her womb despised, insulted, tortured, forsaken, crucified; to hold Him all through life as only hers that she might renounce (not the eternal, inconceivable delight of being His mother, but) the womanly craving for his ease, for His being well esteemed and loved. She would never drag upon Him, she would never afflict Him by pity or self-pity. She would love those who hated Him, because He loved them. She would even love His torments, because they were His will; He had come to suffer.

Victim of our salvation, presented by Mary unto God, vouchsafe to grant our prayer....

Mary, the Immaculate Conception, pray for us.

### FIFTH JOYFUL MYSTERY

### THE FINDING OF OUR BLESSED SAVIOUR IN THE TEMPLE

THE loss of Jesus would fill Mary with distress. Her husband and she for three days sought Him sorrowing. Mary would accuse herself of incredibly forgetting Him; of its being her own fault that He was gone away; but when they found Him, He reminded them that He was man to do God's business; He appealed to their knowledge that it must be so. And then, after this bitter grief, after shaking her soul with terror, after giving this one chance to the teachers of the law of confessing Him their Master, He gave His mother eighteen years of joy: the joy of such a home as earth never before contained, and never will again except in imitation. He gave us the example of a perfect Son, subject to His mother, in youth, through manhood, into middle life; subject not only to His mother, but to His mother's husband, Joseph. Jesus, Mary and Joseph, I give my heart to you.

Jesus, Uncreated Wisdom, have mercy, grant our prayer....

Mary, frightened, sorrowful, and happier than happy, pray for us.

### FIRST SORROWFUL MYSTERY

### THE AGONY AND BLOODY SWEAT OF OUR BLESSED SAVIOUR IN THE GARDEN

BESIDES the revealed knowledge Mary possessed, and the light upon it she had gained by pondering all things in her heart, Mary had lived with Jesus thirty years, and doubtless to such as she He would plainly tell His mind. She knew that "His hour was come and the power of darkness;" and when He went out into the moonlight, she knew that what He went forth to suffer was the vision of sin. God would bring before His agonised Humanity the crimes of every kind that cried to heaven for vengeance, the outraged love of the Creator, the horror of all rebellion, misbelief, ingratitude, uncleanness, and brutality. God would discover to the Son of man the boundless expiation needed, and would lay the weight of all the world's iniquity on Him, wringing Him with anguish. And on the other hand, Satan would be mocking Him with the inefficacy of His propitiation; that in spite of it such millions would be lost, for whom He would suffer in vain.

Jesus, for love of us consenting to that dread agony, vouchsafe to hear our prayer....

Mary, alone in thy heroic sorrow, bearing the woe of thy Beloved, pray for us.

## SECOND SORROWFUL MYSTERY

### THE SCOURGING OF OUR BLESSED LORD

AFTER receiving at the hand of God the weight He came to bear, never to be lifted off His heart till all was consummated, our Lord gave Himself up to His blinded creatures that they might wreak their malice on Him, not knowing, as He pityingly said, what they did, yet knowing that no harm was found in Him, that He had walked among them blameless and merciful, the wonder-worker. Mary knew that the divine wrath was to be satisfied upon her Son in part by the hands of men, to whom "power had been given from on high." Who but the perfect creature, "the woman," the bruiser of the serpent's head, could have conquered herself as Mary did! Along with her shuddering horror at the shame and torment of her Child, there was in Mary a supernatural submission, a godlike patience, a miraculous love for the misdoers, even a certain glory in the mortal agony which a greater tenderness than hers had laid upon her Son and over which His love would triumph; a rapture in the never-sleeping sense that Jesus, her own, the Son of her womb, flesh of her flesh, blood of her blood, whilst the mock of wicked men, and through them suffering the wrath of God, was still, as when He made the worlds, Himself the Beatific Vision.

Jesus, submitting to endure the wrath of God at the hands of creatures, have mercy on us, hear our prayer.

O Mary, by your adoration of Him in His Passion, pray for us.

## THIRD SORROWFUL MYSTERY

## THE CROWNING OF OUR BLESSED LORD WITH THORNS

BESIDES the mortal weight of agony laid on Him by His Father in the garden, Jesus had taken at the hands of men in His scourging the chastisement of all their sensuality. When they took the reed and smote Him on the head, piercing it deep with the great acacia thorns, He, their Creator, gave them power to exact for God the atonement for all sins of pride, self-love, ambition, vanity, conceit, and infidelity. For these the King of Glory wore a crown of thorns.

Jesus, meek and humble of heart, our Atonement, grant our prayer....

Mary, most lowly, pray for us.

## FOURTH SORROWFUL MYSTERY

## JESUS CARRYING HIS CROSS

MARY knew by the shouts of the mob that her Son was on His way to Calvary. She waited for His passing; not to weep over Him, but to gladden Him. An ordinary woman could have so overcome herself as to be full of the same purpose, but only Mary could have cheered the Redeemer at that moment. He came along, faint, weary, goaded, stumbling; spittle and blood upon His face; bleeding, wounded, staggering under the burden He had come to bear; His heart all crushed and wrung with the weight of the wrath of God, with the horror of sin, and of the damnation of the souls that would not be redeemed. But His eyes fell on Mary; and His heart beat high remembering how spotless He had made and kept her by His present suffering; and that she was not only the perfect work of His redemption, but that now, with all this woe before her, she, by the entire conformity of her will with God's, was pressing to His lips the cup of agony, urging Him to drink it to the dregs; inspiring Him for the joy set before Him in the reconciling of the elect, in the justifying of God's love, to endure the Cross, despising the shame, that having loved His own "unto the end" He might sit down satisfied at the right hand of God.

By Thy weariness and faintness, Almighty Lord, have pity, grant our prayer....

Mary, Queen of martyrs, pray for us.

## FIFTH SORROWFUL MYSTERY

## THE CRUCIFIXION OF OUR BLESSED LORD

THE crowd closed round Him, yet for her support God had let Mary see in the gleam on the face of her Son how she had solaced Him. Did she not need that thrill of joy? for she knew the horrors that would go on out of sight before her eyes should again rest on her Beloved, as the awful tree was lifted bearing the Son of God.

Except the Cross, there is no such record of heroic love as the words, "There stood by the cross of Jesus His mother." For Mary was not divine; and, besides all her agony of sympathy and the unutterable strain upon her woman's heart of willing all His torments because they were God's will, all the while she had to take her own farewell. "In peace was her bitterness most bitter." She knew that the humanity He had from her, that "body of death" so ineffably one with hers, was dying now; that in His resurrection and His glory He would indeed for ever be the Son of man, and she His glorious Mother, but that, for ever, that dear, suffering life in which she had fed and clothed, caressed and waited on Him, would be ended, and that in self-sacrifice and faith, and Godlike love of souls, she must annihilate her heart. She must hear His voice give her up to be the devoted, willing mother of her fellow-creatures, His Beloved. "Woman, behold thy Son." Be thou the channel of life and strength to the heroic; the nurse, the tender helper of the weak, the sick, the poor, the sorrowful. To be made thus for ever to the Church what she had been to Jesus, was indeed a glory, but it came with the heart-break that He Himself would no more need her. Her motherhood had been, throughout, a rapture and an agony. She had accepted it knowingly, at the offer of the Archangel. She had accepted it again when she offered her Son in the temple. She had accepted it when He appealed to her knowledge among the doctors. She had accepted it when He left the unimaginable home at Nazareth and "began to preach." She had accepted it when she knew that the hour of His passion was at hand; and now, beneath His Cross, she "stood," herself all swallowed up in Him.

Son of man, forsaken by God, of Thy great mercy, hear us.

Mary, most desolate, pray for us.

## FIRST GLORIOUS MYSTERY

### THE RESURRECTION OF OUR BLESSED LORD FROM THE DEAD

MARY was now to live by faith. Her Son was no longer mortal, but the Conqueror of sin, death, and the grave. He would no longer need her care, her sympathy, or service. She was no more, on earth, to receive from Him the daily caresses and solicitude which had made Nazareth like heaven. Her maternal offices He had made over to the "beloved" for whom He died. Mary had consented to take for her child every soul which Jesus loved and longed for. Godlike still in her conformity of heart, she had been able to promise this because He wished it. Because He loved each soul that should be born into this world with a tender, craving, devouring love, so that to captivate its love He would be fain to die again, she would give herself to every one; her mother's sympathy, her tenderness, her never-failing, sweetest patience, her omnipotence with God. Her life had been a miracle of joy as exquisite as her suffering. Henceforth it would be grayer, more supernatural. To-day she could see Him, the Heart of her heart, and for forty days again; and in the ecstasy of those meetings she would get strength for the mission He bequeathed to her.

Life of all life, vouchsafe to hear our prayer.

Mary, Mother of God, pray for us.

## SECOND GLORIOUS MYSTERY

### THE ASCENSION OF OUR BLESSED LORD INTO HEAVEN

MARY might say to-day, "It is finished." Whilst He came and went, and now and again she could gaze on the divine, beloved face, kiss His dear feet and hands, and see the proof of His humanity in the wounds that had been His death—though all was over she might deceive herself. When the cloud received Him out of her sight, then truly all was finished. Yet Mary did not go back sorrowful. She had not accepted the motherhood of God, and so fulfilled her part, to falter now. Who had the infant Church to look to else? Who but she could tell it of the marvel of the Birth of Christ? Who could so teach it to love Jesus as His mother could? Who else could feed it with His words and deeds? with stories of His Childhood and His Life? Who else could kindle the faint, frightened hearts with love like hers for Him that so loved them, with zeal like His for souls? Who like Mary could persuade them of that love "passing knowledge," "desiring with desire" to be united to them, which had brought God down to take a body from her own? Mary had embraced, with rapturous devotion, the sacrifice of fifteen years of separation, in which she would indeed receive Him sacramentally, and by faith be never parted from Him, but through which her hand should not touch, nor her eye see, Him whom her soul loved. Anything for Him! What were a few years! hardly enough to satisfy her love.

Jesus, gone to the Father, our Way and our Life, vouchsafe to grant our prayer....

Mary, radiant with the joy of sacrifice, pray for us.

## THIRD GLORIOUS MYSTERY

## THE DESCENT OF THE HOLY GHOST

ONCE more did Mary wait for the coming of the Holy Ghost. Once more is Mary overshadowed by the power of the Most High. She, with the infant Church, waited for the promise of the Father; and, in fire, the Holy Ghost, the Comforter, came down. It was thirty-four years since Mary had received Him that she might conceive the Word of God. Now He came again, and He would consecrate her for all time the Mother of His Bride, the Church. For the work of this day her Son had come. "I came to send fire on the earth, and what will I but that it should be kindled?" If He had not come, and suffered and ascended, the Holy Ghost had not been sent. But now, the personal Love of the Father and the Son had descended. He was to bring to each soul of man the knowledge of the intense, devouring love of God for it. He was to teach all hearts that what God asks is a return of love; and to enable them to give to Him a love like fire, consuming "wood, hay, stubble," and purifying self and creature love. O Mary, Bride of God, the fire of love was the very life of all your life. All it could possibly do now was to burn away any mere naturalness in your heart, that from henceforth you should live by faith alone; and that living, as God had done on earth, for souls, you should grow daily dearer to the Father, Son, and Holy Ghost, till once more "it is finished."

O God the Holy Ghost, proceeding from the Father and the Son, have mercy on us, grant our prayer.

Mary, Queen of the Apostles, pray for us.

## FOURTH GLORIOUS MYSTERY

## THE ASSUMPTION OF OUR BLESSED LADY INTO HEAVEN

IT is almost past belief that the least shadow of regret should fall on Mary's heart when she knew that she was passing to her God; the days of her separation fulfilled; her sacrifice completed; her Delight about to call her home. Who can imagine the delicious peace, the exquisite contentment, of her whole being! For fifteen years she had lavished her sweetest sympathy on those she would leave behind. And when she saw them weeping that they should see her face no more, there was regret in her dear heart that they would need and long for her in vain.

All else was rapture of exceeding bliss, and no heart could have wished to delay her. The light of heaven was on her loveliness, more than angelic sweetness in her beauty; and as the apostles gazed their last on Mary, in the hush of her completed happiness the awe of an unseen Presence fell upon them, which was taking her away. Her espousals were fulfilled in heaven. She was gone, leaving with them, as they fondly thought, that almost worshipped body from which it had pleased God to prepare His own. They would cherish it as what the world contained most precious. But "My thoughts are not as your thoughts," saith the Lord. He would not let the Immaculate see corruption. His "love," His "dove," His "undefiled," should in her body be with Him in heaven.

While they poured out their tenderest, reverential care on what was left of Mary, her soul had been taken up through the ranks of the blessed and glorious, and was again in the arms of her Son; and while they thought that her body still consecrated the earth they had laid it in, that too had been raised on high, and Mary was all perfect with God.

Jesus, our Life, and Lover of our souls, vouchsafe to grant our prayer.

By the joy of your assumption, Mary, pray for us.

## FIFTH GLORIOUS MYSTERY

## THE CORONATION OF OUR BLESSED LADY IN HEAVEN

THE angels are present at the joy of God. When had the like been seen in heaven! Mary was come. Not only blameless, innocent, immaculate, the Bride of God and His mother, but she who, above all, had heard the word of God and kept it; the "valiant woman;" the Queen of martyrs; Mary all love. She had begrudged God nothing, and in His lavish gratitude He would for ever and for ever enlarge her capacity and increase His reward. Out of union with His love for souls, Mary had sacrificed her heart for them; and her recompense should be that He would never refuse her prayer. She had given Him all her heart, and He would always hear her. The Almighty would deny His Bride and Mother nothing. She should be the benediction of her people. And for herself, she was with Him; her Own, her Child, her Beloved, her Darling. She was with Him now in bliss for ever; beloved, approved, and welcomed by the Father, Son, and Holy Ghost. As once she was full of grace, so now she was full of glory, full of peace, of rapture and of joy. Her happiness, her beauty, the delight of God. He looked on Mary, and saw that she was very good. How could a creature hold the consciousness of being the delight of the most Holy Trinity! of knowing that never for one moment had the faintest shadow of fault darkened the sunshine of their approbation. The angels worship her who (created a little lower) has become their Queen. The Blessed thank and praise her. Adam and Eve and all their generations extol "the woman," through whom God was made one with man. Joseph, her husband, glories in her love; and on her ecstasy is set the crown of life, the crown of life eternal.

O God the Father,

God the Son, and

God the Holy Ghost, three Persons and one God, have mercy, grant our prayer.

Mary, love-crowned mother, pray for us.

# A ROSARY OF THE SACRED HEART

WHEN our adorable Redeemer was passing to His Father, in the hour of His Passion when, with strong crying and tears, He asked for us God's highest gift, it was that "They all may be one," "I in them, and thou in me, that they may be made perfect in one."

Man's perfection, by union with his Maker, had been the very object of his creation; and though sin (through the depravity of man's will) had seemed to cause a hopeless separation, God's love and desire were still, as from eternity, set upon the work of His hands. His tender purpose should not be frustrated or fail. And yet, how could the ever-blessed, impassible Godhead be allied to sin and its attendant sorrow? To sin it could not be. Sin is the contradiction of God's essential holiness. But for the saving of all creation, and the redemption of mankind, no other miracle should be impossible. What God would do, neither angel nor man could have imagined. God only could have found the way to satisfy His love. He would secure for us that eternal happiness which, apart from Him, we could never enjoy, at a cost to Himself well nigh incredible; and He would secure it with a perfection God alone could have devised. The Word of God, co-equal with the Father and the Holy Ghost in the eternal Trinity, should assume human nature in addition to His own Divine; He should take no human personality, but in His own Divine Person, as God the Son, He should become human, mortal, passible; that, being God, He might, in mortal flesh, expiate the sin of all. When the fulness of time was come He would save a chosen woman from all touch of sin, and of her substance would accept the flesh and blood whose sufferings (as being His) should be an infinite atonement. That flesh and blood He would raise to the throne of God, for ever to personate us there, "the Firstborn of many brethren," "the Way" to God the Father. That Way was closed, but God-made man would open it.

This is the gospel of our salvation. In this way God has redeemed us. Human nature is now for ever admitted into union with God, and the curse of separation being reversed, it is at each soul's choice to be in Christ supremely blest, or to "reject so great salvation." Our manhood being in God, gives to us all the power to be in Him ourselves, if only we but will. No power of hell can put asunder man and God, for God has joined the two together, and the divine love is for ever drawing souls (as "with the cords of a man") to give way to the love of God. In God there is now a human heart loving Him as we ought to love Him, loving all creatures as we ought to love them. That heart is our example, and (as it were) ourselves in heaven already, the object of God's tenderest love, the hope, the strength of all of us, our power to become the sons of God.

Let us say to that Adorable Heart, "I beseech Thee let Thy love, which is as fire in its strength, and for sweetness as the honeycomb, draw away my heart from all things of earth, that for the love of Thy love I may die to the world, who for the love of my love didst die upon the Cross."

"One thing have I desired of the Lord, that I will require: not health, nor wealth, nor rank, nor worldly home; nor worldly happiness, nor any worldly thing; but one drop of that holy fire, one drop of that heavenly flame, to kindle me and set me all on fire with the love of Thee. O may that love consume and burn away every soil and stain both of the flesh and spirit, and consecrate me for a dwelling for Thyself in love, and consume me for a burnt offering acceptable to Thee. I should fear lest I were asking of Thee some great thing, but Thou hast commanded me to love Thee with my whole heart, with my whole mind, with all my soul, and with all my strength; blessed be Thy name for this command, for it is a command to be eternally blessed. Give what Thou commandest, and command what Thou wilt."

## FIRST JOYFUL MYSTERY

### THE ANNUNCIATION OF OUR LADY

THE Archangel was sent to say to Mary that God had chosen her to be the mother of His Son, and to ask her consent. By her faith and her humility, she was already full of grace and full of God. Humility, the sense of utter nothingness, is fulness of God. Because of these was Mary chosen to be the blessed one of all generations.

"Behold the handmaid of the Lord, be it done to me according to Thy word," was Mary's answer; and the divine espousals between God and man were accomplished in her person.

O love of God, preparing for Thyself a human heart, vouchsafe to hear our prayer....

Mary, the woman of all prophecy, the Bride of God, pray for us.

## SECOND JOYFUL MYSTERY

### THE VISITATION OF OUR LADY

GOD'S love had achieved its amazing purpose. "I have loved thee with an eternal love, therefore have I visited thee." God the Son, in His own Divine Person, was taking a created nature from the substance of the Virgin Mary. Think of the joy of the ever-blessed Trinity in a new glory; for now, God as man was adoring God. Think of our Lady's heart, its glad, gay joy, as she hastened across the mountains; its gratitude, its worship, its ecstasy of believing happiness, its oblation of her whole self to God's ends, sure that, moment by moment, she was giving of her own substance for the forming of the Redeemer's body; sure that God loved her; sure that she was pleasing Him; receiving with calm delight the worship of the unborn Prophet and His mother, knowing that indeed she carried God the Son within her.

O love of God, delighting in the lowly, undoubting, joyous love of Mary, and longing for the same in all men, hear us and grant our prayer....

Mary, in whose person all creation is summed up, pray for us.

## THIRD JOYFUL MYSTERY

### THE BIRTH OF OUR SAVIOUR CHRIST IN BETHLEHEM

WHO can figure to himself the satisfaction of the Divine Heart when, all things being now ready, Christ our Lord appeared among His creatures, as He had planned eternally; needing Mary's arms to nurse Him, Mary's breast to feed Him, her sweet words and looks and kisses to caress Him; God—small, and soft, and weak, and tender, and appealing. The heart of our Lady's Baby was the very centre of the love which was drawing all things to itself. It seemed to be all Mary's; but Mary, perfect and beloved as she was in herself, was dearer still to God as the mother of all living, as the one in whom He united all creation to Himself.

O Heart of God new-born, love that hast made Thyself so lovely for the winning of all hearts to Thee, receive and grant our prayer....

Mary, bright mirror of the tenderest love, pray for us.

## FOURTH JOYFUL MYSTERY

### THE PRESENTATION OF OUR BLESSED SAVIOUR IN THE TEMPLE

"THEY carried Him to Jerusalem to present Him to the Lord." Jesus allowed Himself to be carried to His temple, and the price of redemption to be paid for Him. Afar off, in the arms of the aged Simeon, He presented Himself, the Divine Redeemer, to His co-equal Father; and, burning with desire to avenge God's outraged love, and open the way to the Father, offered Himself with all the intensity of His sacred Heart. Think of its passion of divine adoration. Think how it loved all creatures; how it loved Mary, who was making, with the offering of her Child, a holocaust of her own feelings unto God.

O beloved and tender Heart of Jesus, we adore Thee. Hear our prayer....

Mary, offering your Child and your whole self to God's love, pray for us.

## FIFTH JOYFUL MYSTERY

### THE FINDING OF OUR BLESSED LORD IN THE TEMPLE

"I MUST be about my Father's business." Tenderly did our Saviour feel the trial to His Mother's heart when He left her, and she sought Him sorrowing three days, but for such scourges she was prepared. "Whom He loveth He chastiseth," and His Mother was indeed His Beloved. Loved above all, she must suffer more than all. But think of Mary's rapturous thanksgiving when, after all her tears, and weary, self-reproaching anguish, she regained her Boy, and found Him safe, divine and sweet, sitting in the midst of the doctors, "giving testimony to the truth." Think of her fulness of delight when He came up to her the same as ever, her meek, obedient, caressing, tender Child, her Son, her very own, yet intent upon the business of His heavenly Father. Think of the Heart of Jesus, in this His first public work for God. Think of its divine humility, going back to Mary, giving her no reproof, though she called Him the Son of Joseph, only reminding her that they knew who He was, and should have guessed His occupation.

Heart of Jesus, Example of all virtue, hear and grant our prayer....

Mary, most happy Mother of God, pray for us.

### FIRST SORROWFUL MYSTERY

### THE AGONY AND BLOODY SWEAT OF OUR BLESSED SAVIOUR IN THE GARDEN

WITH eternal foresight, and with lifelong, fond intention, our glorious Saviour entered on His Passion. "Lo, I come to do Thy will, O my God." That will was that He, Jesus, the Son of man, God of God, the Holy One, should pass through and feel, as if it were His own, the torment and the horror of all sin, in expiation of the crimes of the whole world. "And He began to be exceeding sorrowful, even unto death." O Jesus, we bow down our hearts before Thy Sacred Heart, which, in the garden, alone, cried out to heaven with the agony God laid upon it. "See if there be any sorrow like unto His sorrow." We adore that dear, submissive Heart, burning with love for God and man, but wrung with anguish, sweating drops of blood.

By Thine "Hour," and Thine Agony, O Heart of Jesus, hear and grant our prayer....

Mary, consenting to the Agony of your Divine Son, pray for us.

### SECOND SORROWFUL MYSTERY

### THE SCOURGING OF OUR BLESSED LORD

THE sharp, keen pain brings to the sacred, lonely heart of Jesus (heavy with the sorrow God had laid upon it) a crushing aggravation to its woe in the sense of man's self-pleasing recklessness whilst He suffers, and the cruel ingratitude with which, in every age, mankind repays His love. O Sacred Heart of Jesus, I have sinned. I have had my own disgraceful part in the cruel stripes they gave Thee. For my self-love, and gluttony, and sloth, and luxury, Thou, O my God, hast suffered. And I say so, and still indulge myself! How revolting to Thy patient, gracious Heart am I! how hateful my ingratitude! But God forbid that I should persevere in hardness. Awake my wretched heart to make amends to Thine.

Heart of Jesus, meek and humble, our Atonement, grant our prayer....

Mary, striving against nature to be willing, pray for us.

## THIRD SORROWFUL MYSTERY

## THE CROWNING OF OUR BLESSED LORD WITH THORNS

"BEHOLD the Man." Who is that Person clothed with purple in derision, crowned with thorns in cruel mockery, and blasphemously saluted "Hail, King of the Jews"? Who is He?

It is no human person. It is God. God, in His highest act of love. God, in our nature. God, who, to content His love, and to achieve the re-union of creation with Himself, has put on our humanity. "Ecce Homo." Heart of Jesus! Heart of God! was it with gibes, and sport, and spitting that they brought Thee forth? And we have all beheld Thee, and have all passed by, wagging our heads! we, who "to nothingness have added only sin." Forgive us, Lord, hide our shame in Thy greatness; Thy Heart still loves us, for it is the Heart of God. We love Thee, we bow down to Thee, we lay our faces in the dust, we prostrate our whole being at Thy feet.

Jesus, despised, insulted, mocked and spit upon; by Thy silence and the sweetness of Thy patient Heart, hear us and grant our prayer....

Mary, in prayer and bitter tears, pray for us.

## FOURTH SORROWFUL MYSTERY

## JESUS CARRYING HIS CROSS

THE cross upon the Heart of Jesus was His Father's wrath and all the weight of all the woe of man; the grief, the pain, the degradation, false-hood, and despair of all humanity. He carried all the sorrows of that human nature which He had condescended to assume. He carried them to expiate them, and to sanctify them for all who in all time should "look to Him in their plagues." Henceforth the way of suffering is the way of God, the way of salvation. Suffering is the way for all: but it is the bait and attraction for loving hearts. "I will show him what great things he shall suffer for my name's sake."

O divine and adorable Heart of Jesus, adorably, divinely loving Lover of our souls, hear us and grant our prayer....

Heart of Mary, pierced with the sword of love, pray for us.

## FIFTH SORROWFUL MYSTERY

### THE CRUCIFIXION OF OUR LORD JESUS CHRIST

THINK for a moment of the joy of heaven, and then, what heaven must have been the day the Son of God was crucified. Think of the amazement of the blessed angels. They knew no sacrificial ecstasy. In God alone such love existed. "Greater love hath no man than this, that a man lay down his life for his friends;" but the divine love did far more. God took to Him a mortal life for this one end, that He might lay it down again for His beloved, "not as though we had first loved God," or were loveable; for no worthiness, or beauty, or gratitude in the creature, "thankless and sinful utterly;" but for the sake of His own love, incomprehensible as God is incomprehensible.

There was "silence in heaven," and God was all in all while the mystery of His love was consummated. But the intensity of even human love overmasters pain, and had the heart of Jesus allowed itself to feel the rapture of its love's divine satisfaction, it could have known no suffering. No temporary pain, no human sorrow, could have coexisted with that supreme delight. Therefore it was that the manhood of our Lord was "forsaken by God;" and that, as it were alone, the Son of man endured His Passion and the Cross; and, having "loved us to the end," gave up the ghost.

O Sacred Heart of Jesus, "past all finding out," we can but kneel, and worship, and adore; believing what appears impossible.

By Thy Cross and Passion, hear us....

Mother of Jesus crucified, pray for us.

## FIRST GLORIOUS MYSTERY

### THE RESURRECTION OF OUR BLESSED LORD FROM THE DEAD

"I LAY down my life that I may take it again." "I am risen, and am still with you. Alleluia."

Jesus, returning from the dead to men "slow of belief and foolish," triumphant over sin and hell, but not over "hard hearts and incredulity"! O Heart of Jesus, for whom hast Thou died and risen? In this "day of Thy power," what wounds didst Thou not receive in the house of Thy friends! Thou didst come to Thine own, and they did not even know Thee. Heart of Jesus, was it only at the first that frightened souls misdoubted Thee? Art Thou glorified now by those on whom Thou didst lavish love stronger than death, high as heaven and deep as the grave?

Shame on us! we ourselves are of those who will not believe "though one rose from the dead." And yet "Christ is risen indeed;" and our faith is not vain; we are not "in our sins," if only we hold fast to Thee, our Resurrection from sin, from self and from the grave, our Resurrection to joy and to God. "Lord save us, we perish." "Lord, we believe; help Thou our unbelief."

O Heart of God incarnate, our hope, and strength, and life eternal, may Thy miraculous love for us kindle our stupid hearts. Have mercy on us, grant our prayer....

Mary, perfect hearer and keeper of the Word of God, pray for us.

## SECOND GLORIOUS MYSTERY

### THE ASCENSION OF OUR BLESSED LORD INTO HEAVEN

"I GO to my Father, and your Father, to my God, and your God;" and, "I am the Way," "no man cometh to the Father but by Me." "Lord, we will follow Thee whithersoever Thou goest." "Thou art set down on the right hand of the Majesty on high," draw us after Thee. "God, for His exceeding love wherewith He loved us, has quickened us and raised us up, and made us sit together in the heavenly places in Christ Jesus." By Him, our Way, we "have access to the Father." Shame on us if we press not forward, "going from strength to strength," after "the prize of our high calling in Christ Jesus."

Heart of God, in our humanity gone up into the inaccessible light of the eternal glory, draw our hearts up to Thee. We adore Thee, hear our prayer....

Mary, whose heart was all in heaven with your treasure, pray for us.

## THIRD GLORIOUS MYSTERY

### THE DESCENT OF GOD THE HOLY GHOST

HEART of Jesus, we adore Thee, mindful still of us. "I will send the Comforter." O God the Holy Ghost, we adore Thee. Thou art the Power and the Love of God. By Thee we can do all things. We can rise above ourselves; we can live unto God; we can conquer and sanctify ourselves by Him who loves us; we can be faithful to Him come what may; we can give Him love for love. O God the Father, God the Son, and God the Holy Ghost, one God, we adore Thee.

Heart of Jesus, glad in the knowledge of the new life Thou hast won for Thy creatures, we adore Thee, hear our prayer....

Mary, Bride of God, pray for us.

## FOURTH GLORIOUS MYSTERY

## THE ASSUMPTION OF OUR BLESSED LADY INTO HEAVEN

O HEART of Jesus, cutting short the sacrifice of Mary, and opening to her (the first, and type, and sum of Thy beloved) the gate of heaven, we adore Thee in the rapture of that day. She came up from her exile, all fair and beautiful within and without, most lovely with love, her heart the perfect copy of the Heart of God; and looking upon her He loved her, and she knew it and was joyful, and her joy was the joy of God.

Heart of Jesus, receiving Thy Mother into Thy bliss and glory, vouchsafe to grant our prayer.

Mary, admitted to the Beatific Vision, pray for us.

## FIFTH GLORIOUS MYSTERY

## THE CORONATION OF OUR BLESSED LADY IN HEAVEN

"A THRONE was set for the King's Mother, and she sat on His right hand; and the King said to her, 'My Mother, ask; for I must not turn away my face.' She was clothed with the sun, and the moon was under her feet, and on her head a crown of twelve stars;" and "beholding the glory of the Lord with open face, she is transformed into the same image, from glory to glory." What is the glory of all glory? Love; for "love is of God," and "God is Love." He loved us unto death, and He loves us in glory, and He desires this for His beloved: that, like Mary, and through Mary, we may each one be united to Himself in one Spirit, and be with Him, seeing Him as He is and for ever, in joy.

O love of God the Father, we adore Thee.

Love of God incarnate, we adore Thee.

Love of God the Paraclete, we adore Thee.

Mary, the Beloved of God, pray for us.

# A ROSARY IN IMITATION OF OUR LADY

HOW may we best please God in our poor thoughts on the mysteries of our salvation?

There has lived one to whose heart and mind they are more living and more dear than to all else together, be they men or angels. That blessed one is Mary.

God is the giver of all grace. He has made some to be prophets, some apostles, some evangelists, some martyrs; by the various grace bestowed on them. To Mary He gave the united grace of all; and its abundant fruitfulness made her the mother of God.

Lowliness, and faith, and love, were all perfect in Mary; and as "the pure in heart shall see God," so, pondering on divine things, she, the Immaculate, saw them in the unclouded light of God's grace. To do our best to feel as she felt and think as she thought, must be pleasing to God. Let us therefore go through our Lady's Rosary, (the epitome of the Gospel), trying to echo her. We shall fail, by the stupidity and sin of our hearts; but it will be something to have tried.

## FIRST JOYFUL MYSTERY

## THE ANNUNCIATION OF OUR LADY

WE may imagine that, at the end of a day of homely work and happiness, Mary, the young wife of Joseph, the carpenter of Nazareth, Virgin of virgins, was alone in prayer; and she might say: "O my Lord, who alone art our King, Thou knowest that Thy handmaid hath never rejoiced but in Thee, O Lord, the God of Abraham" (Esther 14:3, 18). "My heart is ready, my heart is ready," "I will sing to the Lord God of Israel." "My heart hath uttered a good word, I speak my works to the king." And Gabriel appeared and saluted her, being sent to offer to her the motherhood of God: "The Holy Ghost shall come upon thee, and the power of the Most High shall overshadow thee, and the Holy that shall be born of thee shall be called the Son of God, and the Lord God shall give unto Him the throne of David His Father, and He shall reign in the house of Jacob for ever, and of His kingdom there shall be no end." And that blessed Virgin did but say again: "My heart is ready;" for joy and also for sorrow; "be it done to me according to Thy word." But who shall intermeddle with her joy! joy that the hour was come for which all creation groaned; joy that now, for the glory and delight of God and man, the inseparable union of Godhead and manhood should be accomplished; and joy that the marvel, the bridal of heaven and earth, should begin in her!

## SECOND JOYFUL MYSTERY

### THE VISITATION OF OUR LADY

MARY arose in haste, and, as she went across the hills, the humble, happy bride of God, that hymn was "singing in her heart," which her lips poured forth when Elizabeth saluted her, "Mother of my Lord."

Thank God that He has preserved to the world for all time the perfect creature's picture of her soul. We see her irrepressible delight in the choice that God had made of her. We see her joy in her own nothingness. We see her inspired sense that God in that conscious nothingness had found place for the fulness of His love. We see the confident, confiding assertion of her own love and blessedness and glory.

Was the "Magnificat" the expression of a passing rapture? No; it was Mary's life-long temper, its spirit ran through her life. In her most piercing agonies this joy and triumph were underlying all. Mary, like all of us, was an embodied will. That will she offered utterly to God. Her will was to love God wholly; without reserve, without distraction, without admixture, without a thought of self; for she was full of grace, and the Lord was with her, and she knew it, and was glad. At a far distance we can copy this; we can say to our Lord: "My will is to love Thee utterly." Pardoned, and in the grace of God, we can, by His help, fill all the common actions of our daily life with this purpose, and God, with immeasurable love, will fill the hearts from which self is thus cast out. He will set up His palace of delights in the kingdom offered to Him thus, and the humble soul shall extol God's gifts to her, and His work in her, and its life shall be a song of "Glory be to God."

## THIRD JOYFUL MYSTERY

### THE BIRTH OF OUR BLESSED LORD

O MARY, who may rightly honour thee whose heart could say: "My Son, and the Son of the Most High, the Son of God? My little Child is my Redeemer. His Flesh was mine. His Blood was mine. This is the Holy that inhabiteth eternity, my very own sweet Babe and God!" The high prerogative of motherhood is Mary's grace alone. The Incarnation of the Word is the end for which she was created, and no other has been created that could have been Mother of God. But, thanks be to Him, not for her alone did He become her Son. For me, for every soul as if there were no other, He took flesh. There is none but may and ought to claim Him. "A Child is born to us, unto us a Son is given," that thereby God, the Mighty, might win our hearts. He came for each, one by one; loving each with a complete, perfect love, and each, as if no other soul existed, should kneel before God's manger-cradle with the cry: "My very own sweet Babe and God. I have nothing. I am nothing; but I lay my heart and my will at Thy feet. Be Thou my All in All."

## FOURTH JOYFUL MYSTERY

### THE PRESENTATION OF OUR BLESSED SAVIOUR IN THE TEMPLE

WHAT may have been the thoughts of Mary on that fortieth day when Jesus had to be redeemed in the Temple? In simple obedience to the custom of the law, she had prepared the doves, or pigeons, that poor wives were to offer for their purification, and the sum appointed to buy back the first-born of the poor; and then she and Joseph took up Jesus to the temple, but only to the outer court, for they could not enter farther though Mary was the living house of God, and Jesus, God Himself. Might not the blessed Virgin have doubted thus:—"Being the Bride and Mother of God, shall I not dishonour Him by acting as if Joseph were His real father? Being a spotless Virgin, Mother only by the overshadowing power of the Most High, will it not be a false (and even perhaps blasphemous) humility to act as if unclean? Is not my Jesus the Sanctifier of the sanctuary? Am I not, by God's grace, more pure than the new-fallen snow?" But there is one safe answer in all questions—Obedience. Mary knew the law her Son confirmed: "Whatsoever they say unto you do." She never questioned; she submitted. She was not bidden to proclaim her prerogatives. She was silent. She left God's glory to his own good care. She obeyed. Can we not copy her in this. We have no sanctity to hide; still we are often tempted to show off such gifts or goodness as we may possess, and we say that it is for God's glory. We thereby fall into a thousand snares of conceit, and vanity, and scruples. The safety from all such is obedience. Or we are tempted to look solemn and behave peculiarly, to make it known that we are spiritual or pious persons. If we would wish to be like Mary, let us unite our hearts to hers when she appeared in the house of God as unclean, though she, the Immaculate, bore in her arms the well-beloved Son of God.

## FIFTH JOYFUL MYSTERY

## THE FINDING IN THE TEMPLE

IF our poor hearts can realise the anguish of our Lady's tearful cry, "Jesus, my Son, my Son!" as she went about, and lay down, and rose up, for three days seeking Him and sorrowing, they will rejoice in her delight when her sorrow was turned into joy and she found her Treasure in the temple. If our Lord withdrew Himself from His Mother, and hid Himself from her, every one of us must expect the like. If He make His presence sensible within us and let us taste the wonder of His love, the delight is not safe for earth. Now is our only time for sacrifice, for works of love, for patience, courage, faith. He hides Himself, He makes as though we had lost Him quite; that, fearing, longing, trusting, loving, we may call upon the Name of the Lord, we may "search diligently until we find," and seek Him at His altar in His holy house; for it is written, "When thou shalt seek there the Lord thy God, thou shalt find Him; yet so if thou seek Him with all thy heart, and all the affliction of thy soul;" yet not forget to seek for Him within us, for "the kingdom of God is within you."

Jesus came back to His Mother. So will He do to us. He went home with her; obeyed, caressed, and cherished her. So will He do to every one of us, according to the measure of our love and humility. He will return and bring His reward with Him; and the trial of His former disappearance will enhance sevenfold the rapture of His conscious presence.

## FIRST SORROWFUL MYSTERY

## THE AGONY IN THE GARDEN

THE years of Mary's happy home were over. Her joys had been beyond all measure sweeter than any joy this earth had ever known. Now she must bare her soul to the sword which was to pierce it through her Beloved. Jesus went to enter on His Passion, and Mary must not "cry or strive" to have it lightened.

That which, as God, He willed, though she may know the shrinking of His human nature, she must will; though it be to the rending asunder of soul and body. She must know that her own, her Jesus, is taking upon Him a torment which is wringing the very blood through His pores, and she must acquiesce in the depth of her heart. When His nature as man cries out, "Father, let this chalice pass from Me," her spirit must reply to God, "Not what I will, but what Thou wilt." Alone He wrestled with His agony, and she with the bitterness of her heart; and alone we must fight our battle, and die alone. Yet not alone, for the "valley of the shadow of death" He has sanctified by His agony, by the horror of sin (the sting of death) which He then endured in our stead. God may, for the trying of faith, seem to leave a soul helpless, desolate, and frightened; but Jesus Christ alone could endure to die "forsaken."

O believe it, souls which God created. At no time is He more near, more tender, than when He ordains this desperate test, and feigns to desert a soul. He watches, yearning, lest it falter and He lose it. He longs, as a lover does, that the beloved may prove her love by trusting His. If she bears up bravely, waits in faith, calls upon His dear Name, who shall tell the divine delight of the divine, unfathomable Heart! Who shall guess its beating, in the joy of receiving love for love!

## SECOND SORROWFUL MYSTERY

### THE SCOURGING OF OUR BLESSED LORD

O MARY, how didst thou endure this day and live! to know the sacrilege it saw; to bear it, and not die! and they who did those deeds were men; not fiends, but men redeemable, for whom Christ pleased to suffer. Mother, thine eyes could not see, thine ears could not hear the outrage, but what must be thou knewedst in every tortured nerve; loving the Victim adoringly as God; tenderly and passionately as thine own flesh and blood. Amid thy shuddering sobs, Mary, what didst thou implore of God? "Father, save Him from this hour? But for this He came unto this hour. Father, glorify Thy name." Surely God was glorified indeed that day when, besides the obedience of His co-equal Son, He was so loved by a mere creature. Mary, how couldst thou be so God-like! thy heart is with His heart in deadly agony, but yet thy love is as His love. In Him love fought with agony, and He rejoiced in torments which wrought out so great salvation. Unto "the end" He must love on. God must be glorified and man redeemed. But who shall name the awful price? "By His stripes we are saved." Like Mary we must adore this awful mystery, worshipping the inconceivable love which could only thus be satisfied, heart-broken for our share in the agony He took, hating and renouncing wholly every sin our conscience knows, and those we are too bad to see, for all of which our gracious Saviour suffered on that day.

## THIRD SORROWFUL MYSTERY

### THE CROWNING OF OUR BLESSED LORD WITH THORNS

DIDST thou hear those mocking shouts, mother of sorrows, "Hail! King of the Jews"? Had He told thee with what a crown they should insult Him "in the power of darkness"? "Behold the man," manhood itself, God and man in one. The second Person of the most Holy Trinity stood in that crowded court, and not one soul revered Him. They bent the knee in mockery; they wound the thorns of sin around His head with laughter, and they spat on Him. But He was there for love of them, and His love faltered not. But "the woman," she from whom He had received that body of death, knew Him, and waited without in her anguish. Was it not a miracle that thy life could bear the struggle in thy heart and soul, Mary? Each moment of His passion cutting through thy mother-heart, and all the while an ecstasy of adoration, for that He, thy Jesus, is so peerless, so beautiful in His sweetness, so adorable in His meekness and divine in His love. O mother, thou art wonderful, that thou canst endure the cold, indifferent objects of such love. Mother, we know our worthlessness, help us while yet we have the time, to pour our hearts out before Him in worship of the unspeakable perfection of His wondrous love, to break our hearts for having failed to know and care for Him supremely. Help us now to choose Him only for our one good thing, the object of our lives, the desire of our eyes, the love of our love.

## FOURTH SORROWFUL MYSTERY

### JESUS CARRYING HIS CROSS

THE yells of the multitude cannot fail to reach thee, Mary;—"Crucify Him, crucify Him;" and thou knowest that so they will. Mother, thou must forth to meet Him, to satisfy thy love and His. Thou shalt meet Him in the highway of the Cross, that way of holiness which He is consecrating in His blood, by His weariness, His faintness. From henceforth and for all, the way of the Cross is the way of Jesus and the way to God. It is the contradiction of our will, and whether it be in much or little, of one sort or another, it is the token of our Lord and the way of salvation. There is no sort of sorrow in which Jesus will not meet us if, like Mary, we go forth to look for Him. If love inspires us to seek Him, He is already on His way to us, longing that we should come. She sought Him for one mutual, yearning look of love and faith and grace unspeakable; and, in exchanging it, her Lord, her Life, was recompensed. But she was Mary, the perfection of creation. What of us, the miserable failures? Glory be to God and His incomprehensible love, He will even feel Himself repaid if we, the stupid and unfaithful, can find it in our hearts to seek Him in the way of sorrows. O my God, who would not wish to repay Thee!

## FIFTH SORROWFUL MYSTERY

## THE CRUCIFIXION OF OUR LORD JESUS CHRIST

THE procession of death passed on, and Mary after it. "Let us also go, that we may die with Him." In the strength of their mutual love she followed on to Calvary, and waited till the end, crucified with her Beloved, lost to all sense of self and of the horror round her; her life "hid with Christ in God;" her soul absorbed in His death-agony, in His heavenly love and triumph; for here, upon the shameful tree, He triumphed over hell and all its power, and over human sin and weakness; and restored us, every one, to the love of our Creator. The love of God was centred on humanity as Jesus Christ our Saviour hung between the earth and heaven. In Him, man gave to God a perfect glory, and God saw that, in Christ Jesus, man, His crowning work was "very good."

And Mary "stood beside the Cross." It is the central vision of all time—God, giving His only begotten Son to the death of the Cross; and (in the person of our Lady) all creation gasping "Fiat!" in its misery, although its very heart be pierced with the remorse of love. It remains that we, like Mary, be crucified in heart with our Lord; dead indeed unto sin, dead to the world and all its empty pleasures and distractions; dead to self and all its paltry wills; for faith, for gratitude, for love, and through the grace of Him who died for us.

## FIRST GLORIOUS MYSTERY

## THE RESURRECTION OF OUR BLESSED LORD

IT would be hard for dust and ashes to imagine the heart of the Mother of God as she waited for the first day of the week. She prepared no spices, for she knew that her Son would raise Himself from the grave, and that the women would not find Him there. Virgin of virgins! she knew that as His Birth had left her inviolate so the sealed rock could be no hindrance to His Will. No mistrust could she know; only desire, only love, only longing, for His visible triumph; only delight, and gratitude, and love, when it was accomplished.

Only to think upon her joy is joy. She must have looked so beautiful. And now—how her loveliness must brighten if we remind her of the morning when her Joy returned, and He kissed her with the kiss of His mouth; kissed the traces of the tears of her sympathy, and called her His own Mother still.

He was her resurrection and her life as He is ours; but she was sinless, and we have to rise from the deep pit and slough of sin.

In the strength of the grace of Him, our Resurrection, we have to live henceforth like Mary. "We are able." The Feast of the Resurrection, Easter, to the Christian implies communion; and communion, the Lord in us, is strength for everything; strength to live henceforth like Mary, strength for the aim set before us all: "Be ye perfect as also your heavenly Father is perfect;" and as "we can," by His indwelling, rise to this new life, so we are bound to do; no excuse, no delay. "I can do all things in Him who strengtheneth me."

## SECOND GLORIOUS MYSTERY

### THE ASCENSION OF OUR BLESSED LORD

AND what is the secret by which we, like Mary, can lead a risen life? Simply this: "If you be risen with Christ, seek the things that are above, where Christ is sitting at the right hand of God." Our treasure is there, in God. Let our heart be there also. But "above" need not mean above the firmament, nor "the right hand of God" such heaven as we may attain to hereafter—"the kingdom of heaven is within you." Jesus, our treasure, has His chosen home in our hearts. To live our common drudgery of every day—bearing its daily weariness, its petty, unguessed sacrifices, its apparent unsanctity, its unlikeness to what we may think ourselves fit for, its want of sympathy and help—trusting that He is near, seeing the unseen, feeling the unfelt, making His presence (known by faith) our sanctuary from sinful nature, our contemplation, our judge, and our delight: this is to have our life "hid with Christ in God," to be in harmony with Mary, and in union with Jesus Christ. This may be in the busiest or the gayest life of duty. O Mary, pray for us that the rest of our lives we "may so discern God's presence with us and in us, that we may do this and all to His honour and glory."

## THIRD GLORIOUS MYSTERY

## THE DESCENT OF THE HOLY GHOST

IT is not uncommon for Christians so to live as if the old reply were true, "We have not so much as heard whether there be a Holy Ghost." How different was it with our Lady! With what adoration she must ever have remembered the work the Holy Ghost had done in her! With what longing she must have waited for His promised advent after the Ascension! With what meekness of assured, confiding love she must have received the token of the fiery tongue!

Have we received the Holy Ghost? Do we rely upon His help? In our baptism he reversed the curse, and took possession of our hearts. In confirmation He renewed and added to His gifts. We might have gone on daily, like the Blessed Virgin, adding strength to strength by His aid, but we have forgotten and despised Him. We have made our vows to Him, and broken them. Shall we not ask His pardon, and never more forget Him? He is that very Love of God without whom we are cold and selfish. He is the strength of our weakness, by Whom we can conquer sin and Satan. From Him is Grace and Unction, the very breath of our life. He is (in union with the Father and the Son) our Lover, tender, pitiful, and patient. Let us promise reparation of the past for all the days we have to live; and when we say the Gloria Patri let us remember to salute adoringly the Holy Ghost, our Sanctifier, Co-eternal and Co-equal with the Father and the Son in the one all-loving Godhead.

## FOURTH GLORIOUS MYSTERY

## THE ASSUMPTION OF OUR LADY

MARY'S last hour in this world arrived; and how did her heart feel? Ask your own. The moment of death is that of the particular judgment. At that moment, as the soul leaves the body, it is before its Judge: Jesus, the Son of man. The soul stands bare before Him; and every thought and word and deed in the flesh is recalled, and judged by the man Christ Jesus. How did Mary feel? can we venture to remotely guess? When her spiritual eyes were opened to "behold the Man," whom did she see? The adoration of her life. The One to whom as God her whole existence had been consecrated, the One whom, as her child, her Saviour, she had loved tenderly, absorbingly, devouringly, with all the delight, self-devotion, and admiration, of which a creature could be capable. She had vowed herself to Him, had lived for Him, had suffered with Him, longed for Him. Now He had come for her; and her life, as it was unrolled before Him, was one unbroken benediction, one changeless interchange of perfect love. In everything she had pleased Him, and she pleases Him for evermore. In body and soul she is now and for ever in the joy of His presence; the hope of the elect in peril, and of the holy dead.

Most happy Mary, pray for us, that we who have loved ourselves, and known Him late, and loved Him poorly, may, thinking of the joy of thy death, "begin now to serve God a little," so that we too may "love His coming," and the hour of death be our desire, our safety, and our joy.

## FIFTH GLORIOUS MYSTERY

## THE CORONATION OF OUR BLESSED VIRGIN MARY

O SWEETEST Lady, we can only give thee joy of happiness, of rapturous delight such as we but feebly dream of. On earth thou didst receive such ecstasy as we have never even distantly approached; and there lives no soul amongst us who can conceive thy heaven. We can dimly follow thee on earth, believing, if we cannot realise, the sweetness of the sanctity of that life which was so simple. We can a little make our own the sympathy, the sorrow, the pathetic resignation, the silent unutterable woe of all thy suffering with thy Son; but this is past, sweet mother. Thy dolours were but short; eternal are thy joys. We are sad, we suffer often in body and in mind; we can more naturally dwell upon thy martyrdom and realise thy weariness, and faintness, the deadly aching pain of head and limbs and heart, which the torment of love overmastered. But these are swallowed up, thanks be to God, in victory, in the triumph of thy Son and thine in His. And lovest thou not more, my sweetest mother, that we should give thee joy of thy joy? of that which is the everlasting fruit of all the bitterness of earth? does not that contemplation lift our hearts above our present trials, and give us hope and courage, and the foretaste of the brightness of a salvation we expect through thee by Jesus Christ? Happy we, if we can only keep thee in our minds, and live in the remembrance that, with God in His eternal bliss, thou art "our sweetness:" for in thy person we, poor human creatures, are already in the joy of God. Our human nature sits upon His throne in the Person of the Son of God; but in thee is our human personality received into His everlasting bliss. Thou art the Bride of God. But, beyond words inferior as we are, worse far than nothing by our sins, He also calls us, calls us still, to that unspeakable felicity. In thinking of thy bliss we recollect our own; "the joy that is set before us;" we are roused to cleanse our souls and make them ready for the marriage feast; to bathe them in the blood that maketh virgins; to put on the raiment clean and white; to sanctify ourselves by sacraments, and by a pure intention; that when the cry is heard: "Behold the Bridegroom cometh," we may be glad and ready, and may be admitted to the joys "eye hath not seen nor ear heard," which are awaiting all that accept His salvation, in the heavens where Mary is Queen in her joy.

The day we see God in His glory, well pleased with us at last, we shall see her too, our lovely mother; and she will smile and welcome us; and fear will vanish in delight. If such a day be really possible for us, "what manner of people ought we to be now in holy conversation and godliness?"

Printed in Dunstable, United Kingdom

78867888R00060